Glen Huey's Illustrated Guide to
BUILDING PERIOD FURNITURE

THE ULTIMATE STEP-BY-STEP GUIDE

POPULAR WOODWORKING BOOKS
CINCINNATI, OHIO
www.popularwoodworking.com

ABOUT THE AUTHOR

Glen has been active in woodworking for over 30 years. He is the author of *Fine Furniture for a Lifetime* and *Building Fine Furniture*, and he is a contributing editor with *Popular Woodworking* magazine. He is focusing on woodworking education with a series of project-specific DVDs (Woodworker's Edge), seminars, and classes, but he enjoys the challenge of creating new projects for a faithful following of much appreciated customers.

Distributed in Canada by Fraser Direct
100 Armstrong Avenue
Georgetown, Ontario L7G 5S4
Canada

Distributed in the U.K. and Europe by David & Charles
Brunel House
Newton Abbot
Devon TQ12 4PU
England
Tel: (+44) 1626 323200
Fax: (+44) 1626 323319
E-mail: mail@davidandcharles.co.uk

Distributed in Australia by Capricorn Link
P.O. Box 704
Windsor, NSW 2756
Australia

Visit our Web site at www.popularwoodworking.com for information on more resources for woodworkers.

Other fine Popular Woodworking Books are available from your local bookstore or direct from the publisher.

10   09   08   07   06   5   4   3   2   1

Library of Congress Cataloging-in-Publication Data

Huey, Glen, 1959-
  Glen Huey's illustrated guide to building period furniture/Glen Huey.--1st ed.
      p.   cm.
  Includes index.
  ISBN-13: 978-1-55870-770-2 (hc: alk. paper)
  ISBN-10: 1-55870-770-0 (hc: alk paper)
  1. Furniture making--Amateurs' manuals.   2. Furniture--Reproduc-tions--Amateurs' manuals.   I. Title: Illustrated guide to building period furniture.   II. Title.
TT195.H85   2005
684.1'04--dc22   2005027630

METRIC CONVERSION CHART

to convert	to	multiply by
Inches	Centimeters	2.54
Centimeters	Inches	0.4
Feet	Centimeters	30.5
Centimeters	Feet	0.03
Yards	Meters	0.9
Meters	Yards	1.1

ACQUISITIONS EDITOR: Jim Stack
EDITOR: Amy Hattersley
DESIGNER: Brian Roeth
TECHNICAL ILLUSTRATOR: Len Churchill
FINISHED PROJECT PHOTOGRAPHERS: Tim Grondin and Al Parrish
PRODUCTION COORDINATOR: Jennifer L. Wagner

F+W PUBLICATIONS, INC.

ACKNOWLEDGEMENTS

My thanks to:

My wife Laurie; she continues to inspire me. Everyone at Popular Woodworking Books. Leonard Marschark, for his knowledge of clocks. Special thanks to my patrons, Mr. & Mrs. Brad Kasper and Mr. & Mrs. James Foulke. And to my customers, thank you for allowing me to continue down this path.

DEDICATION *To the woodworkers that keep the art of handcrafted furniture alive, well and thriving!*

Read this important safety notice

contents

INTRODUCTION
page 6

SUPPLIERS
page 126

INDEX
page 127

PROJECT ONE 1   **PROJECT TWO** 2

MASSACHUSETTS
BLOCK-FRONT CHEST
page 8

MASSACHUSETTS
HIGH CHEST
(HIGHBOY)
page 24

PROJECT THREE

PROJECT FOUR

PROJECT FIVE

PENNSYLVANIA
CHEST ON CHEST

page 48

PENNSYLVANIA
TALL CASE CLOCK

page 66

NEW ENGLAND DESK
AND BOOKCASE

(SECRETARY)

page 92

THIS IS THE BOOK THAT I HAVE REALLY WANTED TO WRITE! These are the pieces that I dreamed about when I started woodworking. I hoped that when I became a serious woodworker I would build furniture of this magnitude.

I study the pieces at museums and read the best-known books on furniture, but I am not a scholar of the subject. I do not attempt to build pieces that are exact copies of the originals. I try to incorporate the techniques that are time honored and to build furniture with the tools that I have at hand, be they machinery or knowledge. My hope is for you to see how I approach these wonderful pieces and gain aid on your journey in building them.

These pieces, in my opinion, represent the best of their styles of period furniture. Sure, you can find selections with more carvings or more notoriety, but included here is the crème de la crème concerning style. The block-front is a masterpiece in form; it exhibits certain construction techniques that are found in no other furniture. The understated carving of the high chest allows the form to stand out — grace and power in the same glorious piece. The desk and bookcase include some of the most involved aspects of the overall design. A fitted, cathedral interior and tombstone doors bring a particular spotlight to this selection. The chest on chest commands your attention with the fluted quartered columns and pierced hardware. And the clock! This piece takes the standard grandfather design with a broken arched pediment to the next level with the addition of the fretwork and carved mouldings. These five pieces are the benchmark by which others are measured.

MASSACHUSETTS BLOCK-FRONT CHEST

Block-front pieces may be the most sought-after American furniture style today, and the chest is the quintessential design. This sculpted gem from the Chippendale period is a superb example of what American craftsmen could deliver when challenged to move away from the more austere, flat fronts of the Queen Anne tradition.

Most major furniture centers built a version of the block-front chest, but this design was standard in the New England area, around Boston, Massachusetts. Specific features set this piece squarely in that region. The large dovetail that joins the two pieces of the bottom and the blocks that originate in the feet and terminate in the top are but two of these features.

Considered a round-blocked chest of drawers, this Boston beauty is a challenge to build and a triumph when finished. This is a great way to step to the next level in case construction!

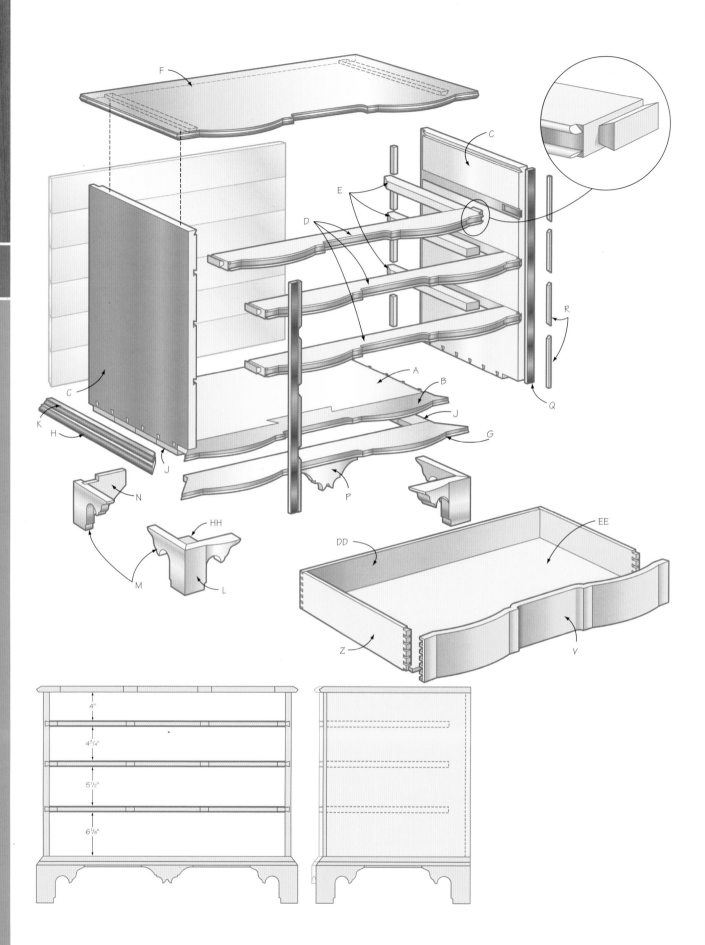

4"

4³/₄"

5¹/₂"

6¹/₈"

inches (millimeters)

REFERENCE	QUANTITY	PART	STOCK	THICKNESS	(mm)	WIDTH	(mm)	LENGTH	(mm)	COMMENTS
CHEST PARTS										
A	1	case bottom	secondary	3/4	(19)	19	(483)	36	(914)	
B	1	case bottom front	primary	3/4	(19)	4 3/4	(121)	37 1/4	(946)	
C	2	case sides	primary	13/16	(21)	20 5/8	(524)	24 1/8	(613)	
D	3	drawer dividers	primary	13/16	(21)	3 1/2	(89)	35 5/16	(897)	dovetail both ends
E	6	drawer runners	secondary	13/16	(21)	1	(25)	17 1/2	(445)	
F	1	case top	primary	13/16	(21)	22 1/2	(572)	38	(965)	
G	1	bottom front moulding	primary	1/2	(13)	3 1/2	(89)	38	(965)	
H	1	bottom side moulding	primary	1/2	(13)	2 1/2	(64)	25	(635)	makes two pieces
J	2	bottom spacers	secondary	1/2	(13)	1 3/4	(45)	24	(610)	
K	1	side moulding	primary	3/4	(19)	2	(51)	24	(610)	makes two pieces
L	1	front feet	primary	1 1/2	(38)	5 1/4	(133)	16	(406)	makes two feet
M	2	side feet	primary	7/8	(22)	5 1/4	(133)	16	(406)	makes four feet
N	1	rear foot	secondary	3/4	(19)	5 3/4	(146)	15	(381)	makes two feet
P	1	drop pendant	primary	3/4	(19)	2 1/2	(64)	7 1/2	(191)	
Q	2	front faces	primary	1/2	(13)	11/16	(18)	23	(584)	
R	2	front face beading	primary	1/8	(3)	1/2	(13)	30	(762)	
DRAWERS										
S	1	top drawer front	primary	2 1/4	(57)	4	(102)	34 1/4	(870)	
T	1	second drawer front	primary	2 1/4	(57)	4 3/4	(121)	34 1/4	(870)	
U	1	third drawer front	primary	2 1/4	(57)	5 1/2	(140)	34 1/4	(870)	
V	1	bottom drawer front	primary	2 1/4	(57)	6 1/8	(156)	34 1/4	(870)	
W	2	top drawer sides	secondary	1/2	(13)	3 7/8	(98)	19	(483)	
X	2	second drawer sides	secondary	1/2	(13)	4 5/8	(118)	19	(483)	
Y	2	third drawer sides	secondary	1/2	(13)	5 3/8	(137)	19	(483)	
Z	2	bottom drawer sides	secondary	1/2	(13)	6	(152)	19	(483)	
AA	1	top drawer back	secondary	1/2	(13)	3 1/8	(79)	34 1/4	(870)	
BB	1	second drawer back	secondary	1/2	(13)	3 7/8	(98)	34 1/4	(870)	
CC	1	third drawer back	secondary	1/2	(13)	4 5/8	(118)	34 1/4	(870)	
DD	1	bottom drawer back	secondary	1/2	(13)	5 1/4	(133)	34 1/4	(870)	
EE	4	drawer bottoms	secondary	5/8	(16)	21	(533)	34 1/4	(870)	cut to size
FF	1	case back	secondary	5/8	(16)	23	(584)	35 5/16	(897)	many pieces
GG	8	drawer stops	secondary	1/2	(13)	5/8	(16)	3	(76)	
HH	4	stacked glue blocks	secondary	3/4	(19)	1 1/2	(38)	12	(305)	seven pieces per foot
JJ	2	side glue blockings	secondary	3/4	(19)	3/4	(19)	12	(305)	2 1/2"-long (64mm) pieces

HARDWARE & SUPPLIES

8 antique-finish drawer pulls, Horton Brass H-81

4 antique-finish drawer escutcheons, Horton Brass H-81E

Using the plans on the DVD, make the plywood template for the drawer dividers. The radius for the round portion of the piece is 15¾" (400mm). The radius for the inside portion is ¾" (19mm). Set up and lay out one half of the template.

Reset the pattern and make the other half of the template.

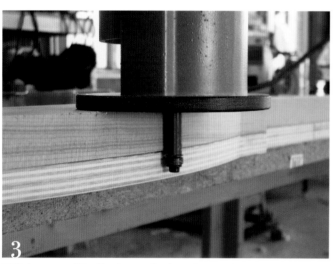

Mill the material for the drawer dividers, then use the template to mark the profile. Cut close to the profile with a band saw, leaving a small amount to trim. Position the pieces as shown and trim them to the final shape with a bottom-mount bearing pattern bit and a router.

Use a ½" (13mm) rabbeting bit set to cut an ⅛"-deep (3mm) rabbet and place that cut directly in the middle of each drawer divider.

This is a ⅛" (3mm) corner beading bit on which I have increased the bearing size one step so that it will cut leaving ⅛" (3mm) of material. Set the bit to profile each edge of the drawer dividers.

Begin the work on the case. Mill the case bottom to size, then lay it out and create the pins.

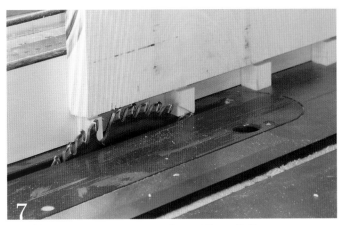

Trim ⅛" (3mm) off the pin area as shown. This will allow you to cover the dovetails with a ¾" (19mm) moulding.

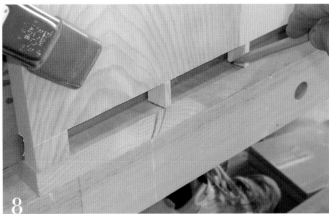

Place the case bottom onto the case sides, aligning the back edges of the two pieces, and transfer the layout onto the case sides. Remove the waste area to create the tails.

Mill the case bottom front to size and make one large dovetail that is 12" (305 mm) long × 1½" (38mm) wide and centered in the piece. Cut the dovetail with a band saw and true up the edges. Next, position this piece to the case bottom by matching the center lines of both and transfer the layout to the bottom. Test the fit, make any needed adjustments, and glue the dovetail into the bottom.

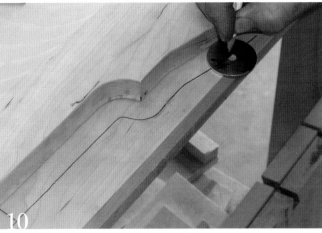

After the piece from step 9 is dry, sand and position one drawer divider to the new case bottom, as shown. The front edge of the rounded portion of the drawer divider should be located ⅝" (16mm) from the front edge of the bottom. Use a pencil in a 1½" (38mm) fender washer with a ¼" (6mm) hole to draw the profile of the front edge of the bottom.

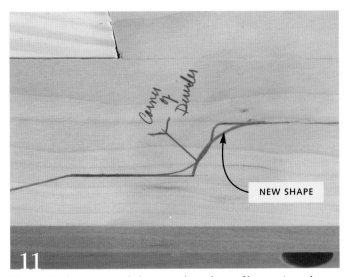

NEW SHAPE

The washer leaves a rounded corner where the profile steps in at the center of the piece. Sharpen this profile as shown.

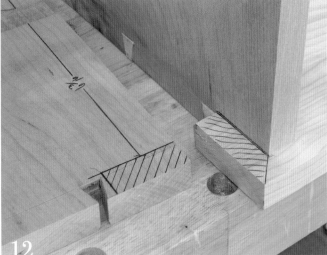

With the bottom edge moulded, slide the case sides into the bottom and mark the 45°-angle cut, as shown. The shaded area is the waste that needs to be removed. Transfer the 45° mark to the underside of the case bottom.

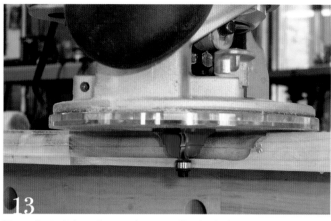

13 Use a classical shaped router bit to profile the front edge of the bottom.

14 Remove the bottom and then flip the piece to make the 45° cut. Attach a straightedge to the underside of the case bottom to help with the cut. Position the saw against the fence and make the first cut.

15 Make the second cut, which will allow you to remove the waste area.

16 Set up the table saw with a stacked dado blade set for a $^{13}/_{16}$" (21mm) cut. Raise the blade to cut $^1/_8$" (3mm) deep. Set the fence to cut at the layout lines that define the drawer dividers. Make the cuts in each case side for each drawer divider, making sure to position the piece in the correct orientation.

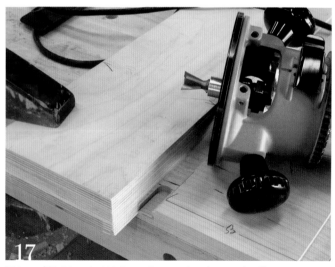

17 Using a $^3/_4$" (19mm), 14° dovetail router bit along with a $^3/_4$" (19mm) outside-diameter bushing, set the fence to $^1/_{32}$" (1mm) past the line of the drawer divider, centering the router bit in the drawer divider area. With the router, run the cut into the case side to a depth of $1^5/_8$" (41mm).

18 Run a half-dovetail along the top edge of the case sides. Bury the router bit in an auxiliary fence so that the bit just cuts into the sides. Cut the pieces on the interior face only. The bit height should be $^1/_2$" (13mm).

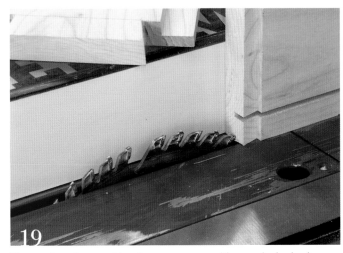

19

To complete the case sides, form a two-step rabbet on the back edge of the case sides. This will house the backboards when you assemble the chest.

20

Turn to the drawer dividers and set up the same router bit used in step 17. To set up the router bit, use a scrap piece that was milled at the same time that the drawer dividers were milled. Once the position is set, cut the dovetail profile on both sides of both ends of the drawer dividers.

21

Remove the back portion of the dovetailed ends, leaving 2" (51mm) of material on the ends. Use the saw fence as a stop. Do this operation on all the ends of the drawer dividers.

22

Remove the top edge of that same dovetailed end. I elected to use my miter saw and set the depth of cut to remove the ½" (13mm) needed. I chose this over the table saw because the miter saw allows me to see the cuts as they are made. Setting a stop block allows you to work directly to the block on each end.

23

Get ready for some assembly. Apply glue to the pins of the bottom and a small amount of glue into the dovetail sockets in the case sides and slide these three parts together. Apply a bit of glue on the drawer divider ends, then insert the drawer dividers into the case. The top edge of each drawer divider's dovetailed end should be flush with the case side. Clamp the pieces until the glue has dried.

24

Mill the case top to size, and set up the dado blade. Adjust the cut thickness to ½" (13mm) and make a straight cut just to the overhang amount. Place the cuts along the ends of the case top, and make them the length of the case sides. Drop-cut one end, and stop-cut the opposite end. To accomplish this, raise the blade to ½" (13mm), and mark the spots where the blade protrudes above the table saw top at the front and back of the blade. Mark these on the fence as shown. Proceed to make the cuts by dropping the front edge of the case top at the line on the outfeed side of the blade, then continue the cut through the top. Begin the opposite cut by pushing the case top through the blade and stopping the cut when the front edge of the case top reaches the layout line on the infeed side of the blade.

25

Load the ¾" (19mm) dovetail bit and bushing back into the router, set a straight-edged fence to a line that is spaced ¹³⁄₁₆" (21mm) from the far edge of the dado cut, then offset the fence ¹⁄₁₆" (2mm) at the back edge of the case top. Essentially this will create a sliding dovetail slot. Make the cuts on the two sides of the case top, and check the fit to the case sides. The case sides will get tighter as you slide them forward toward the front edge of the case. You should just have to tap the final 1" (25mm) or so to tighten the fit completely. If you need to loosen the fit, use sandpaper on the dovetailed edge of the case sides.

Lay the case top onto the bench and position the assembled case so that the front edge of the top extends ⅝" (16mm) to the front. Use a washer the same way you did in step 10 to draw the line of the front edge of the case top. Make sure that the case is centered on the case top.

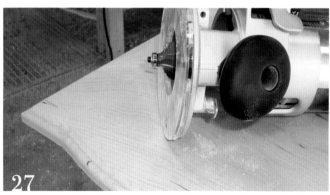

27

Sharpen the marks for interior corners the way you did in step 11. Cut the profile onto the front edge of the case top. Use a classical ogee bit to route the edges of the case top.

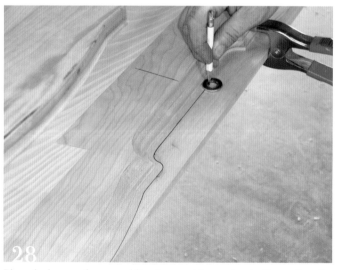

28

Place the bottom front moulding into position under the front edge of the sculpted bottom, and use a pencil and a washer to define the profiled edge. (This is the same setup used in step 26 to determine the case top's profile.) Cut the bottom front moulding and round over the edge with a ⅜" (10mm) bit.

29 Clamp the bottom front moulding to the assembled case. Mark the mitered edge from the sculpted bottom, then cut the 45° cuts with a miter saw.

30 Attach the bottom front moulding to the case with glue and brads. Cut the bottom spacers into pieces of about ½" (13mm), and attach them to the case as shown, again with glue and brads.

31 Move back to the case to install the drawer runners. Mill the drawer runners to size, and make a 45° cut at the rear end of each drawer runner. Predrill the drawer runners as shown. Place a small amount of glue in the first 4" (102mm) of the dadoed area, and attach the drawer runners with nails (1½" [38mm] Horton Brass N-7).

32 Mill the stock for the feet to size according to the cutting list and transfer the foot profile to a piece of plywood for a pattern. Lay out the pattern so that you have two side feet for both the right and left side of the chest, as well as two opposing front feet from the 1½"-thick (38mm) material. Cut and shape the profiles, then drill at the drill press the center area that forms the spur of the foot.

33 Position one front foot on the case and transfer the pattern of the front bottom moulding onto the top of the front foot. Extend a line from the beginning of the rounded section of the front foot to the front edge and down the face as well. This line will be the cut line for the start of shaping the front feet.

34 Set the saw so that the blade is the correct height and the fence is set to make a cut in the waste portion of the front foot. Make the cut into the face of each front foot.

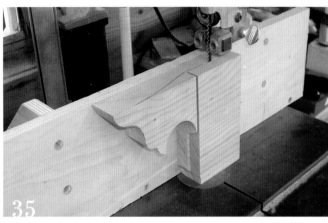

Move to the band saw, set up a straight-edged fence, and make the second cut that will allow you to remove the waste area.

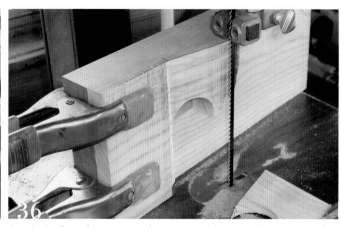

Attach the front foot to a sacrificial piece as shown, and cut the rounded portion of each front foot.

Make the 45° cuts to the front feet and side feet; use the end of the front feet as a starting point for the angle. (See Pennsylvania Chest on Chest, steps 30-32.)

Assemble the rear side feet and the rear feet differently. Cut the rear side feet square at the ends. The joint between the rear side and rear feet is a simple groove that is ¾" (19mm) thick. First, notch the rear feet to fit over the bottom spacers, then assemble the feet and attach firmly to the case bottom.

Profile the side mouldings like the sculpted bottom, and profile the bottom side mouldings like the bottom moulding at the case front. Fit these pieces individually to match the appropriate mouldings, then join the two with glue and brads.

Using a table saw, run a small cut down the first 5" (127mm) of the side moulding. Apply glue to the first 5" (127mm) of the side mouldings and attach them to the case with glue and brads. The saw cut will act as a reservoir to keep any glue from squeezing out onto the case sides.

Repeat these following steps for the two front foot assemblies: Apply glue to the top edge of the foot assembly, position it on the case, and apply a few strategically placed clamps until dry.

While the glue on the feet is drying, make the blocking for the feet. Cut some scrap stock into $1\frac{1}{2}$" × $1\frac{1}{2}$" (38mm × 38mm) pieces and glue them as shown. Rotate every other piece to change the grain direction; this stabilizes the blocks for climatic changes. I like hot hide glue for this process but yellow wood glue will work just fine.

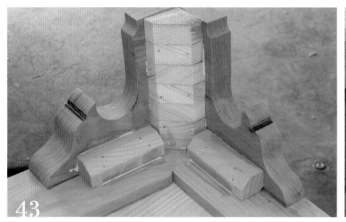

When the glue is dry, cut the blocking to size and attach it to the feet with glue and brads.

Cut the drop pendant at a band saw, sand the edges, and attach the piece to the bottom front moulding directly at the center of the chest.

Get ready for some handwork! Trim the ends of the drawer dividers to 45° to match up with the front face beading. In order to make the cuts, cut a 45° angle on a piece of scrap wood, position it on the case as shown, and carefully trim the angle with a sharp chisel. This process is repeated six times: once each for the top and bottom edges of the three drawer dividers.

46

Attach the case top to the case. Apply glue in the half-dovetailed edge of the case sides and slide the case top into position. There should be a tight fit at the front, and you may need to glue a wedge at the back of each rear side to tighten the joint at the rear of the case. Because the grain in the case top and the grain of the case sides run in the same direction, they will move together during seasonal moisture changes.

Cut the front face pieces to size, and fit them to the case. The face of the pieces should be flush with the center area of the drawer dividers and have a snug fit between the case top and the case bottom.

47

48

Mill the material for the front face beading, and profile the edge with the ⅛" (3mm) corner beading bit. Fit the front face beading to the front of the case. The pieces fit between the 45° cuts in the drawer dividers, against the front face pieces and tightly on the case sides. Fit the front face beading pieces, sand them and attach them with a small amount of glue. Use a spring clamp until the glue is dry.

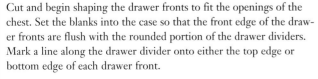

49

Cut and begin shaping the drawer fronts to fit the openings of the chest. Set the blanks into the case so that the front edge of the drawer fronts are flush with the rounded portion of the drawer dividers. Mark a line along the drawer divider onto either the top edge or bottom edge of each drawer front.

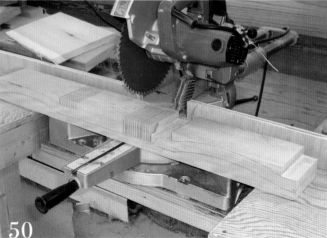

50

This is an old trick that I learned during my home construction days: Set a saw to make kerfs in the waste areas of the drawer fronts, leaving thin pieces of stock. Then break the waste away and clean up to the line.

51

Here's a closer look at the setup in step 50. Using a miter saw, you can see the work as it is being completed; with the table saw the work is hidden against the saw top. Do not make the rounded corner areas. If you want to use the router for cutting away this waste, go after it in stages. Don't cut too deep on any of the passes using the router.

52

Clear away the waste using a chisel. Then use a small plane to smooth to the lines.

53

You can remove the waste at the rounded corners using a band saw, but I have found that using carving chisels is a snap. The #7/20mm sweep gouge fits into the cut just right.

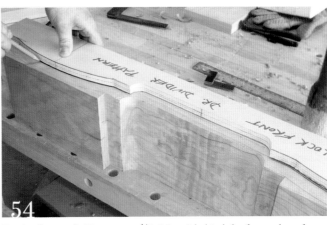

54

Set the drawer divider pattern ¾" (19mm) behind the front edge of the drawer fronts and trace the pattern onto the top edge of the drawer fronts.

55

Make a separate pattern for the inside radius at both ends of the center recessed area. The radius is 1½" (38mm). This pattern will allow you to draw the inner edge of that turn.

56

Make a two-step cut that will establish the squared or blocked area at the ends of your drawer fronts. Make the second cut with the tenon cutting fixture as shown. Use the ¾" (19mm) line as a reference to set the cut.

Set up a band saw with a ½" (13mm), 4 tpi, skip-tooth band saw blade. There is a lot to cut. Cut the curved areas on the faces of the drawer fronts and the entire back of each drawer front.

Shape the rounded fronts. Use a Shinto rasp to do the bulk of the work, then switch to finer rasps and files until you are ready to sand the profile. Work the back of each drawer front to a smooth surface.

Pay close attention to the lines of the block cutouts. Keep them straight as you work the drawer fronts. Using a sharp chisel and a straight edge or small square along with a marking knife will help you shape the drawer fronts. Also, periodically position the drawer fronts into the case and check the reveal around the opening to insure an accurate fit.

Build the drawer boxes. (See Massachusetts High Chest, steps 70-77.) Cut the groove for each drawer front to receive its drawer bottom. (See Massachusetts High Chest, step 82.)

Mill the drawer bottoms to size. Set the drawer boxes in place so that the inside front edge of the drawer front is even with the front edge of the drawer bottom. Mark the profile of the drawer front onto the drawer bottom.

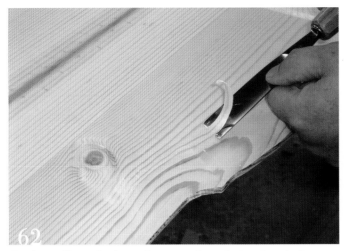

62

Cut the profile on the drawer bottom, and run the bevel on the bottom face of the drawer bottom. I used a shaper, but a raised panel bit in a router table will also work. Because the drawer bottom is ⅝" (16mm) in thickness, the raised-panel profile will leave a rounded edge that needs to be cleaned off for the look of a beveled drawer bottom. Use a plane, a chisel and a sander to smooth the profile. Do not bevel the rear edge of the drawer bottom.

63

Test the fit of the drawer bottom and make any adjustments. While it is in the drawer, make a mark on the drawer bottom at the inside edge of the drawer back. That line will establish the blade height for the cut for the nails that will hold the drawer bottom in position. Make a pass about 10" (254mm) in from each end of the drawer bottom, and attach it to the drawer back with nails after the entire box and drawer bottom are sanded. Add a bit of glue to the groove in the front. (See Massachusetts High Chest, step 84.)

64

Position the drawers in the case and align the fronts so that the reveals are set. Then install the drawer stops using glue and brads as shown.

65

Sand the entire case up to 180-grit sandpaper. While you're finishing the case, make the backboards. (See Pennsylvania Chest on Chest, step 61.) After the case is finished, install the backboards horizontally across the back and join them with half-lap joints.

66

Use a rubber mallet to gently shape the brass drawer pulls to fit the curve of the rounded drawer fronts. Lay the drawer pulls on a scrap that is cut to the same profile as the drawer fronts and gently shape the drawer pulls. After the chest is finished, install the hardware.

MASSACHUSETTS HIGH CHEST

(HIGHBOY)

This design first came to me from customers who were interested in having a high chest built but was wavering between two pieces. Both chests were originally built in Massachusetts and were illustrated by Albert Sacks in The New Fine Points of Furniture: Early American, where they were listed with the masterpiece tag. Either one of these wonderful pieces of furniture would have been a great selection.

Upon talking with the customers I found that they liked certain aspects of each piece, so we designed this high chest to have the best characteristics from each piece. I believe that this highboy turned out to be a "masterpiece" in its own right!

What did the customers think when I finished this piece? They were delighted, and it has become one of the focal points of their collection!

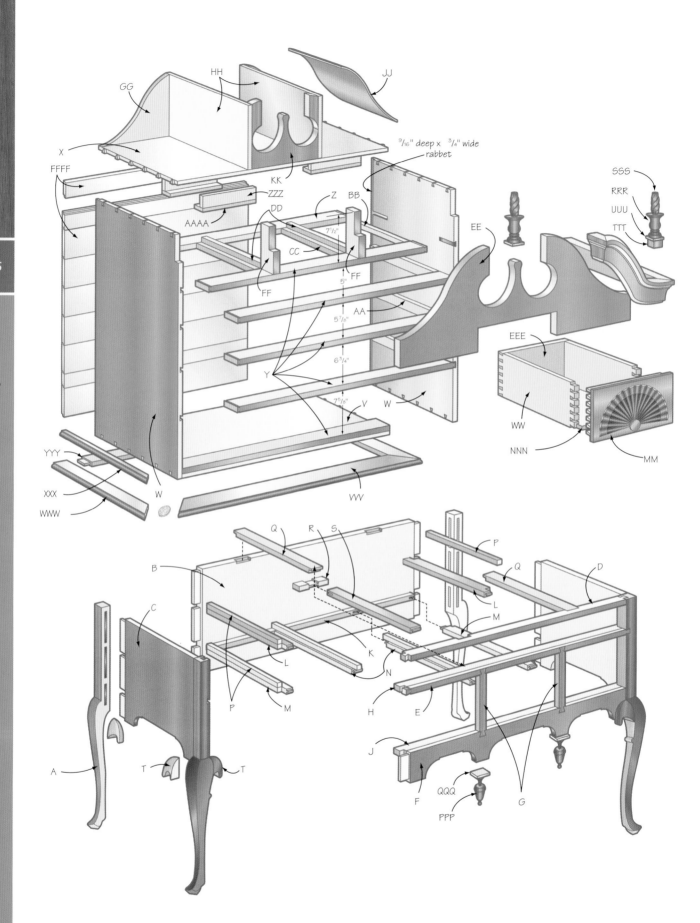

HH

GG

JJ

X

FFFF

KK

ZZZ

AAAA

DD

CC

FF

Z

BB

$7^{1}/_{2}$"

FF

5"

AA

$5^{7}/_{8}$"

$6^{3}/_{4}$"

$7^{5}/_{8}$"

Y

V

W

YYY

XXX

WWW

W

VVV

$^{9}/_{16}$" deep x $^{3}/_{4}$" wide rabbet

EE

SSS

RRR

UUU

TTT

EEE

WW

NNN

MM

Q

R

S

B

C

P

Q

D

L

M

K

N

H

E

L

M

P

A

T

T

J

F

QQQ

PPP

G

inches (*millimeters*)

REFERENCE	QUANTITY	PART	STOCK	THICKNESS	(mm)	WIDTH	(mm)	LENGTH	(mm)	COMMENTS
LOWER CASE SECTION										
A	4	legs	primary	$2^7/_8$	(73)	$2^7/_8$	(73)	$36^1/_2$	(927)	
B	1	back	secondary	$3/_4$	(19)	18	(457)	$38^1/_4$	(972)	$1^1/_8$" (29mm) tenon both ends
C	2	sides	primary	$3/_4$	(19)	18	(457)	21	(533)	$1^1/_8$" (29mm) tenon both ends
D	1	top drawer divider	primary	$3/_4$	(19)	$1^3/_4$	(45)	$37^1/_8$	(943)	$9/_{16}$" (14mm) flat dovetail both ends
E	1	middle drawer divider	primary	$3/_4$	(19)	$1^3/_4$	(45)	$37^1/_8$	(943)	$9/_{16}$" (14mm) dovetail both ends
F	1	front apron	primary	$3/_4$	(19)	$4^1/_4$	(108)	$38^1/_4$	(971)	$1^1/_8$" (29mm) tenon both ends
G	2	vertical drawer dividers	primary	1	(25)	$1^1/_{16}$	(27)	$9^7/_8$	(251)	
H	1	divider extension	primary	$3/_4$	(19)	1	(25)	$37^3/_4$	(959)	
J	1	apron extension	primary	$3/_4$	(19)	2	(51)	$37^3/_4$	(959)	
K	1	rear apron runner support	secondary	$3/_4$	(19)	2	(51)	$37^3/_4$	(959)	
L	2	top drawer runners	secondary	$3/_4$	(19)	$1^5/_8$	(41)	$19^1/_2$	(496)	$1/_2$" (13mm) tenon one end
M	2	lower drawer runner ext.	secondary	$3/_4$	(19)	$1^5/_8$	(41)	18	(457)	$1/_2$" (13mm) tenon one end, $3/_4$" (19mm) tenon one end
N	2	lower drawer runner int.	secondary	$3/_4$	(19)	3	(76)	18	(457)	$1/_2$" (13mm) tenon one end, $3/_4$" (19mm) tenon one end
P	6	drawer guides	secondary	$3/_4$	(19)	1	(25)	18	(457)	
Q	2	top drawer kickers	secondary	$3/_4$	(19)	$1^3/_4$	(45)	$20^1/_2$	(521)	$3/_8$" x $7/_{16}$" (10mm x 11mm) rabbet both ends
R	1	bridle joint back	secondary	$3/_4$	(19)	1	(25)	7	(178)	
S	1	center drawer kicker	secondary	$3/_4$	(19)	3	(76)	$19^1/_2$	(495)	
T	6	knee blocks	primary	1	(25)	2	(51)	4	(102)	use cutoffs from the legs
U	1	lower front apron blocking	primary	$3/_4$	(19)	$3^1/_2$	(89)	6	(152)	both blocks
UPPER CASE SECTION										
V	1	case bottom	secondary	$5/_8$	(16)	$20^1/_2$	(521)	$37^1/_2$	(953)	held to front edge
W	2	case sides	primary	$7/_8$	(22)	$21^1/_4$	(540)	$38^1/_2$	(978)	
X	1	case top	secondary	$3/_4$	(19)	$20^3/_8$	(518)	$37^1/_2$	(953)	held to back, $7/_8$" (22mm) difference
Y	5	front drawer dividers	primary	$7/_8$	(22)	$2^3/_4$	(70)	$36^3/_4$	(934)	dovetail both ends except one (bottom divider)
Z	1	rear drawer divider	secondary	$7/_8$	(22)	$2^3/_4$	(70)	$36^3/_4$	(934)	dovetail both ends
AA	8	drawer runners	secondary	$7/_8$	(22)	1	(25)	18	(457)	$1/_2$" (13mm) tenon one end
BB	2	top drawer runners	secondary	$7/_8$	(22)	1	(25)	$16^1/_4$	(413)	$1/_2$" (13mm) tenon one end, 1" (25mm) tenon one end
CC	2	center top drawer runners	secondary	$7/_8$	(22)	$2^7/_8$	(73)	$16^1/_4$	(413)	$1/_2$" (13mm) tenon one end, 1" (25mm) tenon one end
DD	2	drawer guides	secondary	$3/_4$	(19)	$7/_8$	(22)	15	(381)	
EE	1	scroll board	primary	$7/_8$	(22)	$16^1/_8$	(410)	$37^1/_2$	(953)	
FF	2	vertical drawer dividers	primary	$7/_8$	(22)	$1^1/_2$	(38)	7	(178)	dovetail one end
GG	2	rear bonnet frames	secondary	$3/_4$	(19)	$11^3/_8$	(289)	9	(229)	
HH	2	center bonnet frames	secondary	$3/_4$	(19)	$11^1/_2$	(292)	$20^3/_8$	(518)	
JJ	2	bonnet covers	Baltic birch	$1/_8$	(3)	$21^1/_8$	(537)	17	(432)	
KK	1	scroll board blocking	primary	$3/_4$	(19)	6	(152)	9	(229)	makes all pieces
DRAWER PARTS										
LL	2	#1 and #3 drawer fronts	primary	$7/_8$	(22)	$4^3/_8$	(111)	$10^7/_8$	(276)	$3/_8$" (10mm) lip on ends and top
MM	1	#2 drawer front	primary	$7/_8$	(22)	$7^3/_4$	(197)	$14^1/_8$	(359)	$3/_8$" (10mm) lip on ends and top
NN	1	#4 drawer front	primary	$7/_8$	(22)	$5^1/_4$	(133)	$36^5/_{16}$	(922)	$3/_8$" (10mm) lip on ends and top
PP	1	#5 drawer front	primary	$7/_8$	(22)	$6^1/_8$	(156)	$36^5/_{16}$	(922)	$3/_8$" (10mm) lip on ends and top
QQ	1	#6 drawer front	primary	$7/_8$	(22)	7	(178)	$36^5/_{16}$	(922)	$3/_8$" (10mm) lip on ends and top
RR	1	#7 drawer front	primary	$7/_8$	(22)	$7^7/_8$	(200)	$36^5/_{16}$	(922)	$3/_8$" (10mm) lip on ends and top
SS	1	#8 drawer front	primary	$7/_8$	(22)	$3^7/_8$	(98)	$36^{11}/_{16}$	(932)	$3/_8$" (10mm) lip on ends and top
TT	2	#9 and #11 drawer fronts	primary	$7/_8$	(22)	$8^9/_{16}$	(217)	$11^1/_4$	(286)	$3/_8$" (10mm) lip on ends and top
UU	1	#10 drawer front	primary	$7/_8$	(22)	$8^9/_{16}$	(217)	$13^1/_4$	(337)	$3/_8$" (10mm) lip on ends and top

inches (millimeters)

REFERENCE	QUANTITY	PART	STOCK	THICKNESS	(mm)	WIDTH	(mm)	LENGTH	(mm)	COMMENTS
VV	4	#1 and #3 drawer sides	secondary	$1/2$	(13)	4	(102)	19	(483)	
WW	2	#2 drawer side	secondary	$1/2$	(13)	$7^1/4$	(184)	19	(483)	
XX	2	#4 drawer side	secondary	$1/2$	(13)	$4^7/8$	(124)	19	(483)	
YY	2	#5 drawer side	secondary	$1/2$	(13)	$5^3/4$	(146)	19	(483)	
ZZ	2	#6 drawer side	secondary	$1/2$	(13)	$6^5/8$	(168)	19	(483)	
AAA	2	#7 drawer side	secondary	$1/2$	(13)	$7^1/2$	(191)	19	(483)	
BBB	2	#8 drawer side	secondary	$1/2$	(13)	$3^1/2$	(89)	19	(483)	
CCC	6	#9, #10, #11 drawer sides	secondary	$1/2$	(13)	$8^3/16$	(208)	19	(483)	
DDD	2	#1 and #3 drawer backs	secondary	$1/2$	(13)	$3^1/4$	(83)	$10^1/8$	(257)	$3/4$" [19mm] less than side sizes
EEE	1	#2 drawer back	secondary	$1/2$	(13)	$13^3/8$	(340)	$6^1/2$	(165)	$3/4$" [19mm] less than side sizes
FFF	1	#4 drawer back	secondary	$1/2$	(13)	$4^1/8$	(105)	$35^{11}/16$	(906)	$3/4$" [19mm] less than side sizes
GGG	1	#5 drawer back	secondary	$1/2$	(13)	5	(127)	$35^{11}/16$	(906)	$3/4$" [19mm] less than side sizes
HHH	1	#6 drawer back	secondary	$1/2$	(13)	$5^7/8$	(149)	$35^{11}/16$	(906)	$3/4$" [19mm] less than side sizes
JJJ	1	#7 drawer back	secondary	$1/2$	(13)	$6^3/4$	(172)	$35^{15}/16$	(913)	$3/4$" [19mm] less than side sizes
KKK	1	#8 drawer back	secondary	$1/2$	(13)	$2^3/4$	(70)	$35^{11}/16$	(906)	$3/4$" [19mm] less than side sizes
LLL	2	#9 and #11 drawer backs	secondary	$1/2$	(13)	$7^7/16$	(189)	$10^1/2$	(267)	$3/4$" [19mm] less than side sizes
MMM	1	#10 drawer back	secondary	$1/2$	(13)	$7^7/16$	(189)	$12^1/2$	(318)	$3/4$" [19mm] less than side sizes
NNN	7	drawer bottoms	secondary	$5/8$	(16)	19	(483)	36	(914)	
PPP	2	drop finials (lower apron)	primary	$1^1/2$	(38)	$1^1/2$	(38)	5	(127)	
QQQ	2	drop finial caps	primary	$1/4$	(6)	2	(51)	$2^3/8$	(60)	
RRR	3	top finial urns	primary	$2^7/8$	(73)	$2^7/8$	(73)	5	(127)	
SSS	3	flame finials	primary	$1^5/8$	(41)	$1^5/8$	(41)	5	(127)	
TTT	3	top finial base blocks	primary	$1^1/2$	(38)	$1^1/2$	(38)	6	(152)	
UUU	3	base block caps	primary	$1/4$	(6)	$1^3/4$	(45)	$1^3/4$	(45)	
VVV	1	transition frame front	primary	$7/8$	(22)	3	(76)	$40^1/2$	(1029)	45° cut both ends
WWW	2	transition frame sides	primary	$7/8$	(22)	3	(76)	$22^5/8$	(575)	45° cut one end
XXX	1	transition frame back	secondary	$7/8$	(22)	3	(76)	$36^1/2$	(927)	1" (25mm) tenon both ends
YYY	7	transition mouldings	primary	$3/4$	(19)	$7/8$	(22)			cut to fit
ZZZ	4	secret drawer hanger guides	secondary	$3/4$	(19)	$2^1/4$	(57)	$10^1/2$	(267)	
AAAA	4	secret drawer supports	secondary	$1/2$	(13)	$1^1/2$	(38)	$10^1/2$	(267)	
BBBB	2	secret drawer sides	pri/sec	$7/8$	(22)	$2^1/8$	(54)	12	(305)	
CCCC	4	secret drawer fronts	secondary	$1/2$	(13)	$2^1/8$	(54)	10	(254)	
DDDD	2	secret drawer backs	secondary	$1/2$	(13)	$1^5/8$	(41)	12	(305)	
EEEE	2	secret drawer bottoms	secondary	$1/4$	(6)	$9^1/4$	(235)	$11^3/8$	(289)	
FFFF		backboards								many half-lap pieces
GGGG	2	top gooseneck mouldings	primary	3	(76)	8	(203)	34	(864)	
HHHH	1	top return moulding	primary	3	(76)	$6^1/2$	(165)	26	(660)	this will make two mouldings

HARDWARE & SUPPLIES

14 antique-finish drawer pulls, Horton Brass CH-7

5 antique-finish keyhole escutcheons, Horton Brass CH-7E

2 $5/8$" (16mm) antique-finish drawer knobs, Horton Brass H-42

clout or shingle nails, Horton Brass N-7

Begin this project by reproducing the leg pattern from the plan section on the accompanying DVD. For this pattern use plywood for rigidity. Mill the lumber for the leg blanks to size according to the cutting list. Do the layout work on each blank, keeping the back edges of the patterns together.

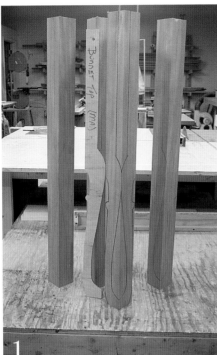

At the table saw, set the depth of cut so that the waste area of the front of the leg is cut exactly along the knee, as shown. This defines the knee and makes the cutting of the leg easier. There are two cuts to be made to each blank. Notice in the picture the knob just below the back of the knee. This needs to remain on the front side of the front legs for carving. I find it better to keep this knob on each leg until I have sculpted the legs to final shape and selected the legs for the front. At that time I remove the knob for the back legs. Mark an X from corner to corner on the end of each blank; this locates the center that will be used for mounting the blank at the lathe.

Load the leg blanks onto the lathe, centering each blank at the X. Here you are going to turn the foot of each cabriole leg. Begin this process by delineating the top edge of the foot. Turn the entire foot, up to that line, round with a gouge. Next determine the diameter and height of the pad, the section below the foot that meets the floor, as well as the diameter where the foot meets the pad. Use a parting tool to establish the two diameters. With a skew, carefully shape the roundness of the foot and the bevel of the pad to their respective shapes. Complete these steps for the foot on each blank.

Move to the band saw to begin cutting the leg blanks. Use a bridge for cutting the first side of the blanks. This is where you cut in from each end of each section that is to be cut, leaving ½" (13mm) of material attached. At the knee, cut into the table saw cut, completely removing the waste material. Use a hot glue gun to stick the waste back into position. These steps will keep the waste areas on the first side attached and the lines for the second side in place. With the first side cut, make the cuts on the second side. This time you can cut the waste completely free from the blank. Finally, move back to the first side and finish the cutting of the bridges and remove the glued-on knee area, leaving a "roughed-out" leg blank.

With the feet shaped, it is time to remove the additional material at the top block of each leg. This can be cut at the table saw, as I have done here; pay close attention to the blade so as not to cut into the leg. You can use the band saw instead to accomplish this step. The goal is to leave a 1⅝" (41mm) square block at the top of each leg. Make two cuts per leg. Remember that these cuts establish the face sides of the leg posts. This step needs to be done after the feet are shaped; you cannot successfully mount the blanks onto the lathe if this stock has been removed!

Shaping of the leg is next. Here it is best to work all legs at the same time if possible. Begin by rounding the ankle — the area just above the foot — to a completely round profile. By using a Shinto rasp, shown here, and other files and rasps, work the leg so that it transitions from round at the ankle to square at the knee. Make this a gradual, smooth transition. Check the legs against one another to make sure that they appear identical. (For additional information, see *Popular Woodworking* magazine, volume 143.)

The next step is to flatten the top of the foot so that the foot transitions into the ankle of the leg. While this can be completed with chisels and rasps, I find that a spindle sander can speed the process. With shaping complete, scrape and sand the leg to a final grit of 150.

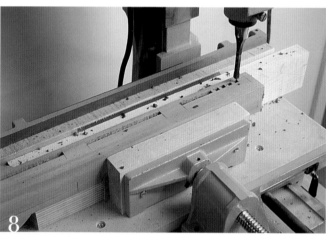

With the legs shaped, choose the best legs for the front. Remove the knob from the back legs. Position the leg orientation, then locate and cut mortises for the aprons. The front lower apron has a single mortise, while the side and back mortises are split mortises so as not to weaken the leg posts. Use a "step" method to cut the mortises (¼" [6mm] wide × 1¼" [32mm] deep), leaving ¼" (6mm) at each end and 1" (25mm) of solid material between the sections.

Lay out the location of the center drawer divider on the inside of the front legs. Use the router with a ¾" (19mm) dovetail bit extended %₁₆" (14mm) into the leg and a ¾" (19mm) outside diameter bushing to create the first half of the joint. Allowing the bushing to ride against a fence will ensure a cut that is centered for the ¾" (19mm) divider.

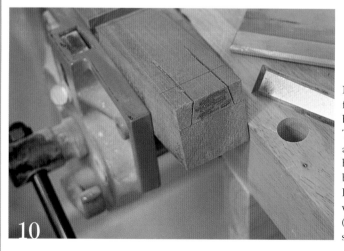

Next, lay out the dovetail socket for the top rail and cut the half-blind dovetail for the top divider. This is best done with a handsaw and chisels, but to make the job a bit quicker you can "hog" out the bulk of the material with a Forstner bit and finish the joint with a chisel. This is a %₁₆"-long (14mm) × ¾"-deep (19mm) socket set into the leg post.

Next cut away the waste areas with a handsaw and chisel. Make sure to oversize the waste areas a bit. The extra space allows the panels to expand in response to seasonal movements without placing stress on the joint.

Turning to the back, the sides and the front apron, create the tenons on the ends of each piece. I find this easiest to do by essentially cutting two rabbet cuts along each end. Make the first cuts on the faces with the blade raised to ¼" (6mm) and the fence set to cut a 1⅛" (29mm) tongue. Make the second cut with the piece standing on end and the blade raised to the 1⅛" (29mm) level. The fence should be set at ½" (13mm) if you are working with ¾" (19mm) stock, as recommended. With the tenons made, set the pieces into orientation with the correct legs and transfer the layout of the mortises to the tenons.

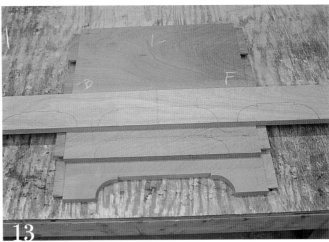

With the tenons created and cut, lay out the decorative patterns for the sides and the front apron from the plan. Make the profile cuts and sand to finish. Dry fit the pieces to check for proper joint.

Mill the top and middle dividers to size according to the cut sheet. Begin with the top rail. Cut dovetails in the top divider to fit into the legs' hand-cut socket that you made in step 10. Use the socket as a template for the dovetail. Then, make a sliding dovetail on each end of the middle divider using the same bit that was used to create the first half of the joint in step 9. (See project three, "Pennsylvania Chest on Chest", step 12 for details.)

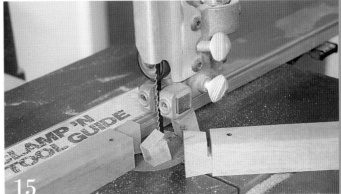

While you are set up for creating the dovetails on the ends of the middle divider, raise the bit to ¾" (19mm) and create that same detail on the ends of the two pieces that will become the vertical drawer dividers. At the table saw, make a cut at the shoulder of the dovetail that is ½" (13mm) deep, then remove the material at the band saw leaving ½" (13mm) of thickness. Some assembly can be completed at this point. Glue, clamp and square the front and back assemblies.

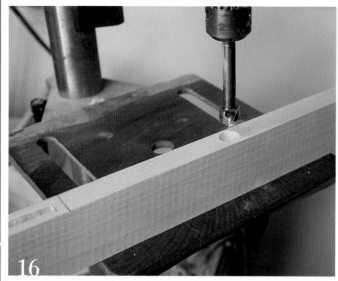

16

Mill the material for the divider and apron extensions, as well as the rear apron runner support. Locate and cut the mortises for each piece. Also, remember the mortise for the center drawer kicker, which is centered in the divider extension. The mortises are $\frac{1}{4}$" (6mm) wide, and they are $\frac{1}{2}$" (13mm) deep for front use and $\frac{3}{4}$" (19mm) deep for rear use. The two front extensions are glued into position while the rear extension is to be attached with nails. Because the piece is 2" (51mm) wide, countersink the hole for the $1\frac{1}{2}$" (38mm) clout nail with a $\frac{3}{4}$" (19mm) Forstner bit.

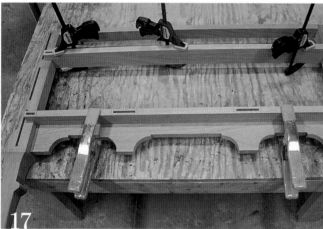

17

Attach the two front extensions only. Here you can see how they are positioned.

18

With the dividers in place, lay out and mark the location of the vertical dividers. Set the pieces into position and transfer the dovetails onto the dividers to create the sockets. Here we return to hand tools. Use a dovetail saw to make a series of cuts that define the socket; make a number of cuts inside the socket as well. With a sharp chisel remove the waste material from the socket and level the bottom of the joint. Check each socket with the matching dovetailed divider until each joint has a snug fit.

19

Prepare the material for the drawer runners. The four runners for the lower drawers get a $\frac{1}{2}$" (13mm) tenon at the front and a $\frac{3}{4}$" (19mm) tenon at the rear. The top drawer runners have a $\frac{1}{2}$" (13mm) tenon on one end. Create all the tenons at the table saw in a two-step method. The first step makes the shoulder cut (material lying flat on the saw top) while the second step, shown here, defines the cheek cut (material standing perpendicular to the saw top). One additional step needs to be performed on the rear of the top drawer runners: Cut a notch on the end of the runner where it will wrap around the rear leg posts.

20

Here you can see the notch needed on the top drawer runners. Now it is time for more assembly. There is a lot to glue here; work quickly, or you could elect to make a number of sub-assemblies. Glue and position the front tenons on all the runners, and slide the rear apron runner support onto the runners. Apply glue to the tenons and mortises of the sides and slip them in place. Finally, apply glue in the tenons of the back assembly and attach the back to the balance of the case.

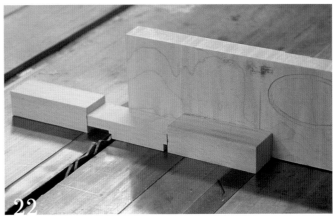

With the lower case assembled, use a square to level the lower drawer runners so that they are level from front to back, and attach them to the back using the wood screws. Mill, cut and fit the drawer guides onto their respective runners and attach them with brads. Attach the top drawer runners to the rear legs with one clout or shingle nail.

Except for the middle drawer, each drawer in the bottom row has a kicker. To keep the drawer from kicking down as you open it, make and install a kicker using a bridle joint. The first step of this simple bridle joint is to create laps on each face of the stock that is to be attached to the case back. Raise the saw blade to ¼" (6mm) and make a series of passes on each face to complete the piece.

Next, cut an open mortise on the end of the kicker. This is made just as the tenon on the runners except that you remove the ¼" (6mm) of material in the center and leave the stock on either side.

Drill with a Forstner bit to countersink the first piece for a 1½" (38mm) clout nail. Apply glue to the mortise in the divider extension and to the tenon on the kicker, slip the bridle joint together, and install the assembly into position. Once installed, level the kicker to the back and attach the bridle joint with nails.

The last step needed to complete the inner workings of the lower case is to install the top drawer kickers. With a rabbeting bit in the router set for a ⅜"-wide (10mm) cut that is ⁷⁄₁₆" (11mm) deep, make two cuts in the top drawer divider and two cuts in the case back that will accept the kickers, about 2" (51mm) wide. Move in a little more than 3" (76mm) from the case sides. Use the same rabbeting bit setup to create a rabbet on both ends of the kicker. Make sure that the top of the kicker is flush with the top edge of the case.

Begin the knee blocks by cutting the pieces to the flat profile provided in the plans. The important aspect of this work is to match the grain on the blocks to that of the legs, especially on the two front legs! Position the profiled piece to the leg and trace the knee pattern onto the block.

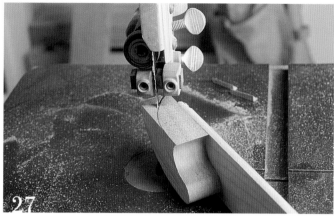

With a single ¾" (19mm) screw, temporarily attach the block to a piece of ¼" (6mm) plywood that is as wide as the block, making sure that the flat side (the side that attaches to the leg) is even with the plywood. At the band saw, carefully cut the shape, keeping the plywood in contact with the saw table. Remember that you will need three sets of mirrored pieces.

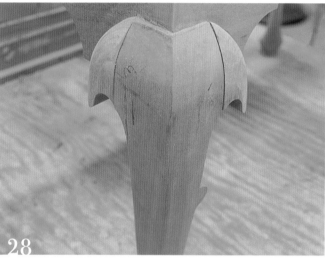

Attach the cut knee blocks to the legs using glue and a brad through the side or apron. I like to use a true hide glue here for the quickness of set as well as the slight gap filling abilities. With the glue set, attach the block with a screw from behind, into the block. Finish with any filing or sanding necessary.

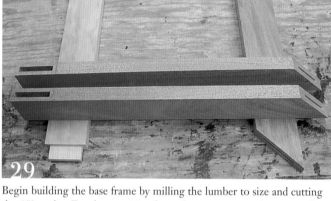

Begin building the base frame by milling the lumber to size and cutting the 45° angles. For the transition frame front, cut one end, measure from the point of that end, and cut the opposite end to the correct length. Then, cut the angle on one end of each side piece, and square cut the opposite end. Mark the center of each angle cut and create a slot for a No.20 biscuit. Cut one end of the rear frame piece square. Lay out the two 1" (25mm) tenons on that same end. Match the piece to the inside of the front piece, aligning the innermost tenon mark with one end of the front piece. Mark where the opposite angle of the front meets the back piece; cut the back piece at that point. This process insures that the base frame will be square. Next, lay out the mortises in each of the side pieces. They are ¼" (6mm) wide × 2½" (64mm) long × 1⅛" (29mm) deep.

Cut the mortises. Create the tenons on the frame parts, then assemble the transition frame by gluing the mortise-and-tenon joints as well as the biscuit-cut front joints. By placing the clamps as shown you can perfectly close and match the angles and tighten the mortise-and-tenon joints. Allow the frame to dry.

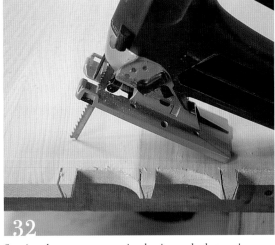

With the frame dry, sand the piece to 150 grit and use a classic ogee bit to profile the top and a small roundover bit on the bottom edge of the sides and front. To attach the frame to the lower section, use No.8 × 1¼" (32mm) flat-head wood screws through the top divider and place ¼" (6mm) slot cuts in the sides and back of the case to use wooden clips. (See Pennsylvania Chest on Chest, step 39.)

Starting the upper case section begins at the bottom! Mark the bottom to create pins for the dovetail joint. With layout complete, create the cuts that define the dovetails then remove the waste either by hand using a chisel or, as shown here, using a jigsaw to remove the majority of the waste then finishing the pins with chisels. Cut the sides of each pin to delineate the joint. Carefully run the jigsaw in one end of the waste area, turn, and move down the scribe line. When you reach the opposite end gently kick the saw back on its heel while holding it still. As the saw kicks back, it cuts to the angle, allowing the waste to drop. Work across one direction on each end, then turn and repeat the process coming back. This will remove the majority of the waste, leaving you to tune up the cuts with chisels.

Set the sides with the face down on the workbench and place the bottom into position with the face side toward you. Reach in and transfer the layout of the pins onto the sides using a sharp pencil or marking knife.

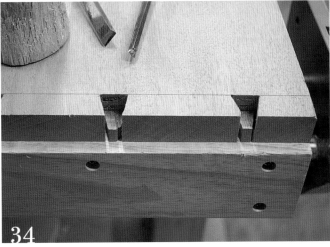

Remove the waste area of the sides (thereby creating the tails), and test-fit the joint. Repeat steps 32-34, creating the pins in the case top, then fitting the case top to the sides. When finished, you will have the box of the upper case section ready.

A couple of operations need to be completed on the case sides. First, book-match the case sides and choose the front of your case. Do the layout work to locate the drawer dividers and the bottom edge of the scroll board. Transfer those lines to the second side making sure that you create a mirror image. Using the straight-edged jig, a ¾" (19mm) dovetail router bit and a ¾" (19mm) outside diameter bushing, make the cuts for the drawer dividers. There are four dovetail cuts at the front edge of each side (the divider that sits directly on the case bottom does not get dovetailed) and one at the back edge of the case sides to accept the runners for the divided drawers in the top row.

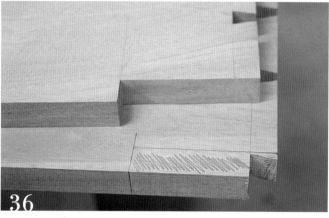

Next, make a $\frac{9}{16}$"-deep (14mm) × $\frac{3}{4}$"-wide (19mm) rabbet along the interior of each case side back edge to house the backboards. Notch the front top edge of each case side to accept the scroll board. This notch is $\frac{7}{8}$" (22mm) deep and begins at the top edge of the top drawers as on the layout. With the upper case box complete, glue the dovetail joints, check for square by cross measuring, and allow the box to dry.

Next, cut the drawer dividers to size, taking the measurement from your upper case box, and cutting on each end the sliding dovetails that fit the cuts made in step 35. Use the same bit you used in that step to make the corresponding dovetails. Remember that you need to create this dovetail on the ends of the rear divider or runner support too!

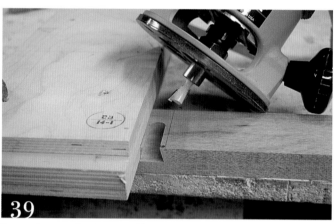

Lay out and cut the mortises for the drawer runners—one mortise at each end of the dividers. Do not forget that the top row of drawers is divided, so you will need to cut those mortises as well. The rear runner support receives a full mortise, where the top drawer divider has a split mortise. (This deviation comes into play in the next step.) The front mortises are $\frac{1}{2}$" (13mm) deep, and the rear mortises are $1\frac{1}{8}$" (29mm) deep.

Set up the straightedge and a $\frac{3}{4}$" (19mm) dovetail router bit to cut a $1\frac{1}{4}$"-deep (32mm) dovetail slot for the vertical drawer dividers in the top bank of drawers. If you were to cut the complete mortise behind this vertical divider you would overly weaken the joint.

It's time to glue in the drawer dividers. Apply glue to the dovetail socket and the dovetail, then set the joint. Remember two things: The mortises go toward the inside of the case, and the top divider is the one that has the extra mortises for the divided drawers. It is easy to get their positions changed. Also at this time, attach the bottom drawer divider, which is cut to fit the case snugly, with a thin bead of glue and screws driven from the underside of the case bottom.

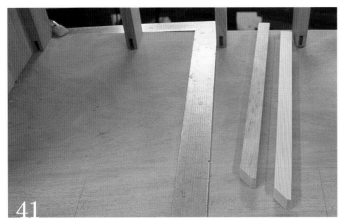

41

Mill the drawer runners to size and create the tenons on the ends (³⁄₈"-long [10mm] on the front and 1"-long [25mm] on the back). I cut the ends of the drawer runners that fit against the case sides with a 45° angle for aesthetics.

42

Cut the tenons on the center top drawer runners and make the extra cuts on the front end. Match the mortise made in the divider in step 38.

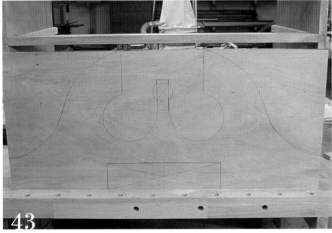

43

Now it is time to design the scroll board. Make a template of the piece from the plans and transfer it onto your board. Also, lay out the area that will be removed for the taller, carved center drawer, which is directly centered. Remove that waste and carefully cut the bonnet detail as well. When the cuts are complete and sanded, set the scroll board to the case top. Do not glue them.

44

Mill the vertical drawer dividers to size and create the dovetail to match the slot made in step 39. Next, notch the dividers to fit around the scroll board. The notch should be ⁷⁄₈" (22mm) deep and begin 4¼" (108mm) above the dovetail shoulder.

45

Here you can see how the vertical drawer dividers get attached to the case. First glue the socket and the dovetail, then apply glue to the front edge of the case top, position the scroll board in place and add one No.8 × 1¼" (32mm) flat-head wood screw in the upper corner of the scroll board where it meets the case top. Finally, hold the vertical drawer divider even with the cutout area of the scroll board, predrill, and countersink two No.8 × 1¼" (32mm) flathead wood screws.

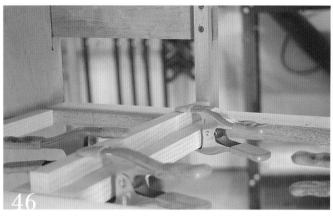

Install the two drawer guides. Place them directly behind the vertical dividers on top of the runners and glue them into position.

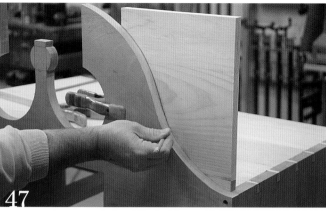

To begin the bonnet, place the rear bonnet frame directly behind the scroll board and resting on the case top. It should be flush with the outside of the case and stop 1" (25mm) from the cutout in the scroll board. With it clamped in place, trace the shape of the scroll board onto the rear bonnet support. Make one for each side, then cut and sand the edges before attaching them to the case top with glue and No.8 × 1¼" (32mm) flat-head wood screws through the underside of the case top.

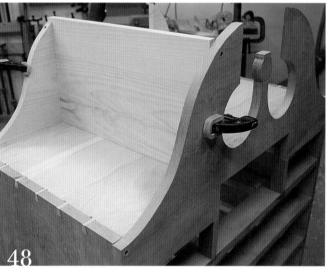

Next, cut the center bonnet frames to size and attach them to both the rear bonnet frame and the scroll board. Use screws and glue blocks to add strength where the frames butt into the scroll board. Once they're installed and the glue is dry, plane the top edges of the center bonnet frames to the slope of the rear bonnet frame and the scroll board.

Add the reinforcement pieces to the scroll board between the center bonnet frames. Trace the pattern onto the pieces, cut them to fit, and glue them.

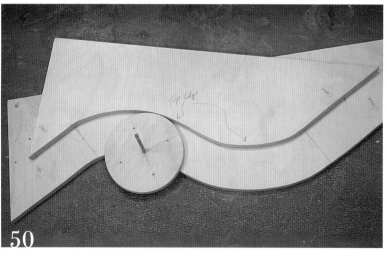

To prepare the stock for the gooseneck mouldings, make a few templates from ½" (13mm) plywood. First make a pattern of the scroll board or the rear bonnet frame and at the ends of the piece make the continuation an additional 6" (152mm) or so. (The top piece is shown.) Cut the profile, and sand it smooth. Next make a circle of plywood with a center hole. For the mouldings that I made for this project, the moulding is 3" (76mm) from top to bottom, so I made the circle with a 6" (152mm) diameter. If your moulding is larger or smaller, adjust the size of the circle accordingly. Finally place the top template into position and, using a pencil in the center of the wheel, mark the profile of the bottom edge of your moulding. Cut this template to be used in the next step.

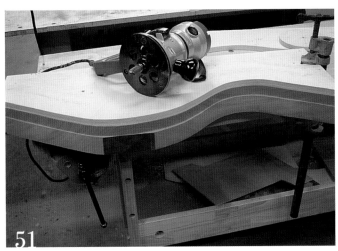

51

Mill the lumber for all your mouldings to the thickness required for your gooseneck. (In this example that thickness is 2⅞" [73mm].) Secure the second template to the stock and use at least a 1" (25mm) cutting-length top-mounted bearing router bit to begin the cut. The bearing will follow the pattern. Be mindful of the grain direction. There are places that you may have to climb-cut to keep from tearing out the material.

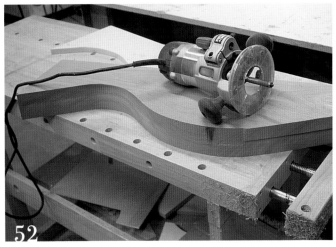

52

Flip the stock over, and use a bottom-mounted bearing bit to complete the cut.

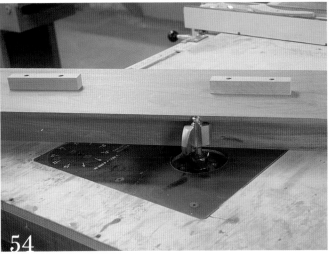

54

Use a set of custom-made router bits for the edge profile on the bonnet mouldings. Shown here is one method of using those bits at the router table. If you do not have a bit set or choose not to have a set made, see "Pennsylvania Tall Case Clock" steps #65-70 for another method.

53

This is important: For the gooseneck mouldings, make sure that you have two pieces of stock that are mirror images of one another. Be sure you have enough material for your side mouldings (see the cutting list) and the short return moulding at the center of the scroll board.

55

This is another method that can be used to create the bonnet mouldings with the router bits. Here the block, cut to the thickness of the moulding plus the thickness of the plywood pattern stock, is attached to the supplemental router base, which is plywood. The combination allows the router to be balanced in accordance with the stock.

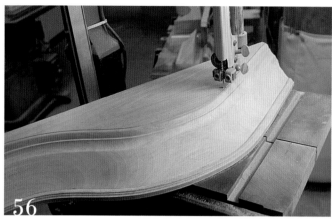

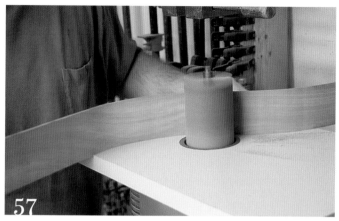

56 Depending on your router set, you might need to hand carve the bead detail that is at the bottom edge of the moulding profile. Do this before cutting the mouldings loose. Once the mouldings are made it is time to cut the pieces from the stock. In cutting the last router passes, set the bit to just nick the profile, leaving a distinct line and revealing the cut line. Carefully cut the moulding from the stock at the band saw.

57 Using a spindle sander, straighten the edge and smooth the cut as necessary.

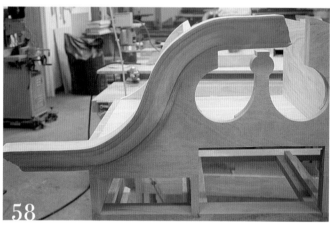

58 Using a couple of screws, temporarily attach the moulding to the scroll board. Orient the moulding to the scroll board to allow ¼" (6mm) of the moulding to extend above the scroll board. Note the amount of extra moulded stock that is available for use on the top returns. Mark the cut lines at the top at the scroll board and at the bottom where the moulding meets the case sides.

59 Use a piece of plywood, shown here attached to the bonnet mouldings, where the outer edges of the plywood are level with the top and bottom edges of the mouldings. Position the set to make the first cut on the mouldings. In this setup, the combination of pieces needs to be spaced away from the miter saw fence. The width of the spacer is equal to the thickness of the moulding stock.

60 Reverse the position of the setup in step 59 — no spacer is necessary — and make the second cut to complete the cutting on the gooseneck mouldings.

61 Reposition the gooseneck moulding by reattaching it with screws, then predrill and nail the moulding into place with finish nails. Place three nails along the length of the moulding.

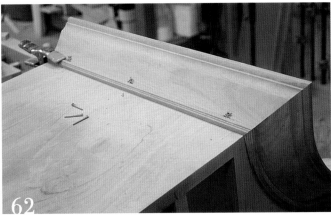

62

63

The returns that are attached along the case sides are next. You can measure and cut these using the miter saw alone. The front corner matches the gooseneck moulding, while the back is straight cut to the rear edge of the case. Some adjustment may be needed in the profiles to accurately effect the match. When ready, use a small amount of glue — 3"- 4" (76mm-102mm) at the front edge — then nail the moulding in place.

Take the same steps to cut and attach the gooseneck returns. I find that using heated hide glue is great in this instance. The glue sets quickly, allowing you to position the piece, and it holds the piece while you install the brads to complete the process. Before I move on I like to make a connection of the returns to the gooseneck using a small piece of dowel. Drill in from the sides of the returns, near the top edge of the moulding, then glue and install a ⅛" (3mm) dowel.

64

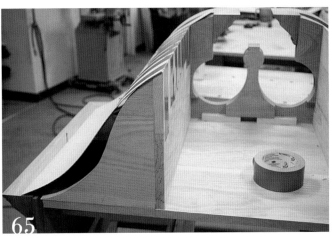

65

Next up are the secret drawers that are located above the top row outer drawers and are accessible only through the area of the top row middle drawer when it is removed. These pieces are attached to the case top with two No.8 × 1¼" (32mm) flat-head wood screws, as shown. Attach the secret drawer supports to the hanger guides, then position the assembly into the case. Draw a line on each side of the assembly, making sure that the piece is perpendicular to the case side. Make a small hole through the case top, with the bit being centered between the lines. Use the holes to locate the screws (No.8 × 1¼" [32mm] flat-head wood screws) used to attach the unit to the case top. Repeat these steps for the second hanger assembly, maintaining the appropriate width for the drawer. Complete the opposite side in the same manner.

Cut the bonnet cover to the correct size using the bonnet framing for the pattern. Add glue to the center frame support and position the plywood, keeping the edge level with that of the frame and tight to the back edge of the gooseneck. Apply duct tape as a clamp. When that is dry, pull the plywood up, add glue and "spring" the piece into position. Add brads as necessary for a tight fit.

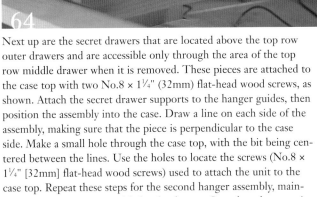

66

Set the upper section onto the transition frame. Create the transition moulding, cut the sides and front to fit around the upper case section, and attach the moulding to the transition frame with brads, being careful not to nail into the upper case section.

67

Begin the drawers by milling the drawer fronts to size based on the openings of the case. Add ⅝" (16mm) to the overall length of the opening and ¼" (6mm) to the overall width of the opening to arrive at the size of each drawer front. Once the fronts are milled, add a ³⁄₁₆" (5mm) roundover profile to each edge. Make these roundovers ¼" (6mm) deep.

At the saw, set the blade height to ⁵⁄₁₆" (8mm) and set the fence ⁵⁄₁₆" (8mm) away from the blade. Make the cut on both ends and the top edge, with the drawer front against the fence. Next, bring the blade height up to the top edge of the cut just made and set the fence ¼" (6mm) from the blade. (Using a ⅛" [3mm] blade you will get a ⅜" [10mm] cut. If you are using a thin-kerf blade, set the fence accordingly.) Use the miter gauge to make the cut at each end of the drawer front. Test the fit by placing the lower edge of the drawer front into the case. You want about a ⅛" (3mm) gap when the drawer front is pushed tightly against one end of the opening. If it looks good, finish the cuts. If you need to, make a slight adjustment, then finish the cuts.

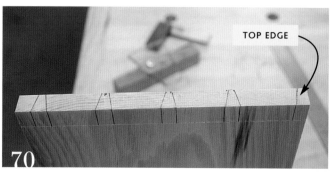

70

Mill the drawer parts to size based on your drawer fronts. Choose the face and top of the drawer backs, then clamp one piece into the vise with the face away from you. Find the top of the piece and using the dovetail marking gauge, draw a line about ¼" (6mm) in from the top edge and extending toward the top and back of the piece. Slide to the opposite end; about ¼" (6mm) from the end, draw a second line that slopes in the same direction as the first. Draw a third line with the opposite side of the marking jig to create and complete the first pin of the dovetail layout. Divide the remaining space equally by placing a small line at the upper edge of the drawer back. Mark other pins by placing the angles of the dovetail on either side of the layout marks. Finally, draw lines from the dovetail layout lines to the scribe line as shown.

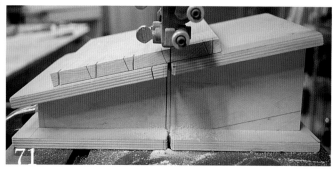

71

Using the dovetail cutting jig at the band saw, cut to the scribe line on the appropriate angle. Cut half of the lines, turn the jig around, then cut the remaining lines.

69

Now, without readjusting the fence or blade height, cut the rabbet at the top edge of each drawer front. Check the fit in the case again by putting the drawer front into the case. You need at least ⅛" (3mm) of clearance for a drawer of this size. Wider drawer fronts require a bit more gap. I like to position each drawer front into the case to check the fit and to see the piece come together.

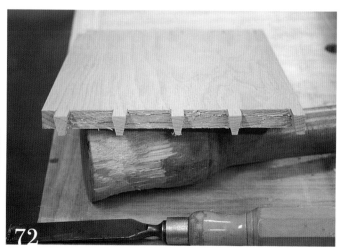

72

Using chisels and beginning with the face side up, remove the waste by locating the chisel slightly in front of the scribe line and setting it with a mallet. Move across the waste areas of the piece. Next cut in from the end and allow the waste to chip out. Repeat this process until you get halfway through the thickness. Flip the drawer back facedown, and remove the balance of the waste material in the same manner.

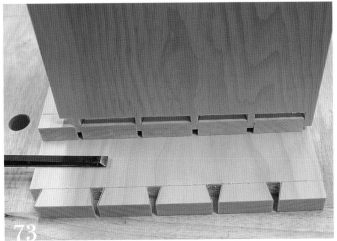

73

Choose the better face of each drawer side and orient the best faces together as a pair. Mark the outside faces of the pair with an X. Select the top edge, as you did in step 70, and mark an X on it as well. Choose which end of the pair will attach to the drawer back. Once you choose, scribe the back with the scribe set to the thickness of the back. Lay one of the sides with the face down and the scribe line toward you. Set the back into place, aligning the top edges. Remember that the face of the drawer back should now face you. Flush the backs to the side piece and, with a sharp pencil, transfer the layout of the pins onto the sides. At the band saw with the piece flat against the table, cut on the waste side of each line. Remember to leave a bit of space between the line and your cut to insure a tight fit. Carefully remove the waste from between the dovetails. Repeat the same steps for the other side piece. Test the fit of the joint. It should be snug but not overly tight. Make any necessary adjustments for fit. Then complete this step for the remaining drawers.

tip

You can remove a large amount of waste while creating the dovetail sockets in the drawer fronts by using an appropriately sized Forstner bit to hog out the waste. Then use your chisels to complete the work.

74

Start the dovetails on one drawer front by placing the piece in the vise with the face away from you. Next, using the dovetail marking jig, create the layout for the pins as you did in step 70. This time, however, lay out one large dovetail with each line set about ¼" (6mm) in from the end. Next divide the large tail into equal smaller tails, as shown, and extend the lines down the front about 2" (51mm). Using a dovetail saw, cut on the waste side of the line. Use the longer straight lines and the angled layout lines as a guide. Cut to the drawer lip, but try not to nick it.

75

Remove the waste areas to create the pins. Begin with the chisel slightly in front of the scribe line, and set the chisel with the mallet. Walk across the tails to the opposite end. Bring the chisel to the end of the drawer front; while holding the tool at an angle to the tail, remove one corner of the waste. Slide to the other end of the waste area; again holding the tool at an angle, remove the second corner. This process allows you to remove the dovetail waste without damaging the sharp angles of the pins. Repeat steps 74 and 75 for each dovetail on each drawer.

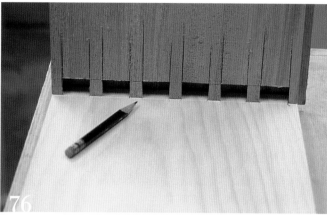

76

Set your marking gauge to the thickness of the rabbet of the drawer front. Scribe the drawer sides to that size, set the sides with the face to the bench, then transfer the dovetails to the drawer sides with a sharp pencil. Create the tails on the drawer sides with all drawers. The drawer boxes are complete, but do not assemble them yet.

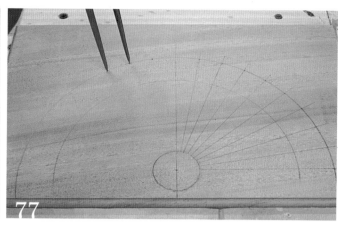

77

Begin carving the fans on the upper and lower center drawers by laying out the shape according to the plans. The outer ring defines the fan, while the inner ring is the deepest cut in the design. When drawing the fan's rays, make sure you run the line well beyond the outer ring.

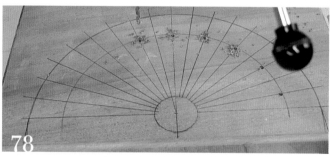

78

At the drill press use a $1/8$" (3mm) bit to drill a hole on every other ray at the inner ring. The depth of each hole is $3/16$" (5mm).

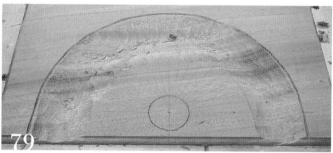

79

Use a No.15, 6mm V-parting tool to define the outer ring of the fan. With that complete, use a No.5, 12mm sweep gouge to remove the waste material from the fan's outer edge, removing an equal amount of material on each side of the drilled holes. This creates a roll into the center at the drilled depth from each direction. Carve in the direction of the grain. It will change as you move around the piece, so make adjustments as necessary.

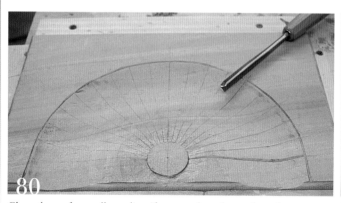

80

Clean the surface well, sanding if you need to, then redraw the ray lines. Using the V-parting tool, cut the lines of the fan's rays to a consistent depth over the entire length of each ray. Be extra careful as you approach the center of the fan: The rays become very fine at that point, and it is easy to chip away material. Next, round over the edges of the fan's rays. I find that a No.25, 3mm back bent gouge works great here.

81

For the upper fan, remove the material at the bottom edge of the fan, below the first and last ray, to a level even with the drawer lip. For the lower fan, remove the material below the first and last rays to a level that is $3/16$" (5mm) below the lip of the drawer. This allows a shadow edge to be presented in the front apron of the lower case section (see step 85). Remember that you did not cut a rabbet on the drawer front's bottom edge. Make the sides of the fan roll down to the proper level, keeping consistent with the balance of the fan. Finally, use a No.2, 8mm sweep gouge to touch up any areas at the fan's edge, leaving a sharp detail around the outer ring. Sand the fan smooth.

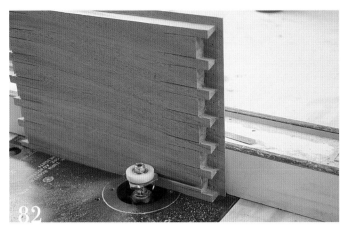

82

It is time to create the groove in the drawer parts that will house the drawer bottom. In the example shown, I am using a three-wing cutter that makes a ¼" (6mm) cut and has a bearing that sets for a ¼"-deep (6mm) cut as well. Make the cut in the drawer fronts and sides with the bit height set at ¾" (19mm). (Pay attention to the lower center drawer front: Because of the depth of carving, the groove may need to be adjusted.) The drawer bottom will enter the back of the drawer just below the drawer back and slide into position within the drawer box. (Remember the ¾" (19mm) difference between the drawer sides and back?) Sand the interior of the drawer boxes to clean up any lines; glue the boxes together, making sure to check for square; and allow to dry. If you use the setup shown, run the piece left to right past the cutter!

83

Mill the drawer bottoms to size, taking the measurements from the drawer boxes. Put a fence extension in place, set the blade to a 12° angle, and set the fence ³⁄₁₆" (5mm) away from the blades just as it dips under the saw table. This setup will result in a beveled edge for the drawer bottoms that will fit snugly into the ¼" (6mm) groove. Raise the blade to cut through the thickness of the bottom, as shown, then create the bevel on three edges. Remember that the grain of the bottom runs side to side; be sure to orient it in that way.

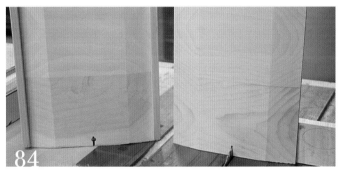

84

Slide the bottom into the drawer box and mark the bottom just at the inside of the drawer back. Remove the bottom from the drawer. Raise the blade to just below that line and make a pass cutting the bottom for the nail that will hold the bottom in place but allow movement. (Wider drawers will need two equally spaced slots.) Sand each drawer bottom, place a small amount of glue into the groove in the drawer front, and slide the bottom into position. At the nail slot, predrill a hole and place a 1½" (38mm) clout or shingle nail into the drawer back.

85

Place the lower center drawer into the case, and mark the bottom edge of the fan carving onto the front apron. That material will need to be carved away to create the shadow area. Use the gouge to carve the area, then smooth it by sanding.

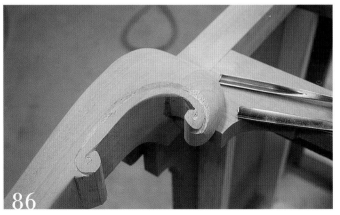

86

Use carving tools to shape the front knee back and leg detail. The scroll begins as a small rosette at the end of the knee block and finishes with the same detail at the knob that was left when you shaped the legs. Draw the design into the leg, and begin with the V-parting tool. Work slowly, carving and watching the grain direction. Once the line is set, slope the balance of the leg into the line using a small gouge. Also, round the edges of the scroll (I like the back bent gouge for this step). Sand the scroll to clean it up and smooth it.

While you have the lower case laid down to carve the scrolls, add the lower front apron blocking, as shown. Position the block behind the apron profile, trace the design onto the block, and cut it to shape. Glue and clamp each piece in place when complete.

87

To make the drop finial caps and the base block caps for the top finials, use a thick piece of stock that is cut to the correct size. Mark each flat side with an *X* to find a center location for drilling. Run the four edges at both the top and bottom with a $\frac{1}{4}$" (6mm) beading bit. At the band saw, slice the finished pieces from the block. (Next, attach the drop finial caps with glue and brads.) For the base block caps, drill the $\frac{5}{8}$" (16mm) hole to accept the top finial urn.

88

With the drop finial caps attached to the edge of the front apron, drill the $\frac{3}{8}$" (10mm) hole for the post of the finial. Take a square block of wood; at the drill press, drill a $\frac{3}{8}$" (10mm) hole through the block. Place the point of a $\frac{3}{8}$" (10mm) brad point bit into the center of the *X* marked in the previous step, allow the block to rest firmly on the cap, and drill the hole. The use of the block will help to keep the hole straight.

89

90

Turn the drop finial according to plan and test the fit — it should be snug! The goal is to have enough of a friction fit that the finial need not be glued, it can just be pressed into the apron.

91

Cut the top finial base blocks to size, drill the hole for the urn post, and position the block into the corner formed by the gooseneck and side mouldings. Using a small square based on the side moulding, hold the block and trace a line along the bottom edge where the block meets the bonnet cover. This small detail will allow your block, urn and finial to stand straight. When this is complete, add a small amount of glue to the base of the block and attach the block to the bonnet cover with a No.8 × 1$\frac{1}{4}$" (32mm) flat-head wood screw. To attach the caps, use a piece of dowel to locate the position, then add glue and a couple of brads to secure them.

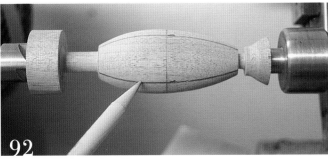

92

Begin creating the flame finials at the lathe. Turn the piece to shape according to the plan. Draw a line around the finial that is centered as shown. To obtain the four equal sections wrap a small strip of paper around the finial. Mark the point where the strip meets the starting edge. Remove the strip and cut at that line. Lay out four equal spaces on this strip. Rewrap the paper and transfer those marks to the turned piece. All that is left is to draw the straight lines at those marks.

93

Starting at the bottom of the finial, draw a line that begins at one section line, turns upward past the second line, and then connects with the third line as it meets the center line of the finial. Continue this line up to the top of the finial. Repeat for each of the four section lines to complete the layout for the flame finials. Each line represents the highest point of the flame. Remove the waste material using a ball bit in a power carver or by hand.

94

Turn the top finial urns to shape according to the plan. Drill a ⅝" (16mm) hole in a scrap piece of wood so that you can position the urn under the bit at the drill press, then cut the ⅝" (16mm) hole into the center of the urn that will accept the flame finial.

95

Trim off the bottom waste of the flame finial and test the fit between each flame finial and its top finial urn. With this step complete, two pieces of each three pairs can be joined.

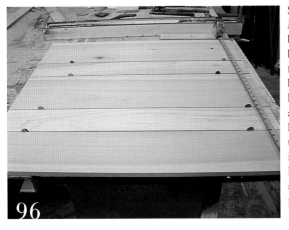

96

Sand the entire project to 180 grit. Make the half-lap backboards for the piece. Mill the material to thickness, and make sure that you have parallel edges on the boards. The length can be determined after you create the half-lap joint. Set the blade height to half the thickness of the backboards, and set the fence ¼" (6mm) from the blade. Make the first cut for the rabbets in one long edge. Flip the boards face for face and make the cut in the other edge. Note that you should have two boards that will have rabbets on one edge only. Reset the blade height and fence position to complete the rabbet. Make sure that when set together the lap joint is both flat and tight. Lay out the boards correctly, and place spacers between each board. (I use one penny in the summer months and two pennies during the winter months.) Measure the size required for the case back, and cut the last piece to the mark. Cut the pieces to the necessary length, and the backboards are ready to use. Do not install them until you have completed the finishing process on the case! (See the accompanying DVD for finishing techniques.)

PENNSYLVANIA CHEST ON CHEST

The general design of the chest on chest can be found in the locations where quality furniture was built in the early to middle 18th century. From Boston to Newport to Philadelphia, each areas had its own variations of the piece.

The most prolific, if not the most outstanding, examples were built in Pennsylvania. The "platform" ogee bracket feet, the fluted and quartered columns in both the upper and lower sections of the case, and the fine and delicate dentil mouldings of the cornice all work to lead your eye toward the center and then travel upward. This emphasizes the verticality of the piece while it is balanced in width.

This chest is based on a piece built circa 1760-1780. With exquisite beading surrounding drawers that bear "pierced" Chippendale pulls, this selection has all the great design features. It should become a part of your furniture collection.

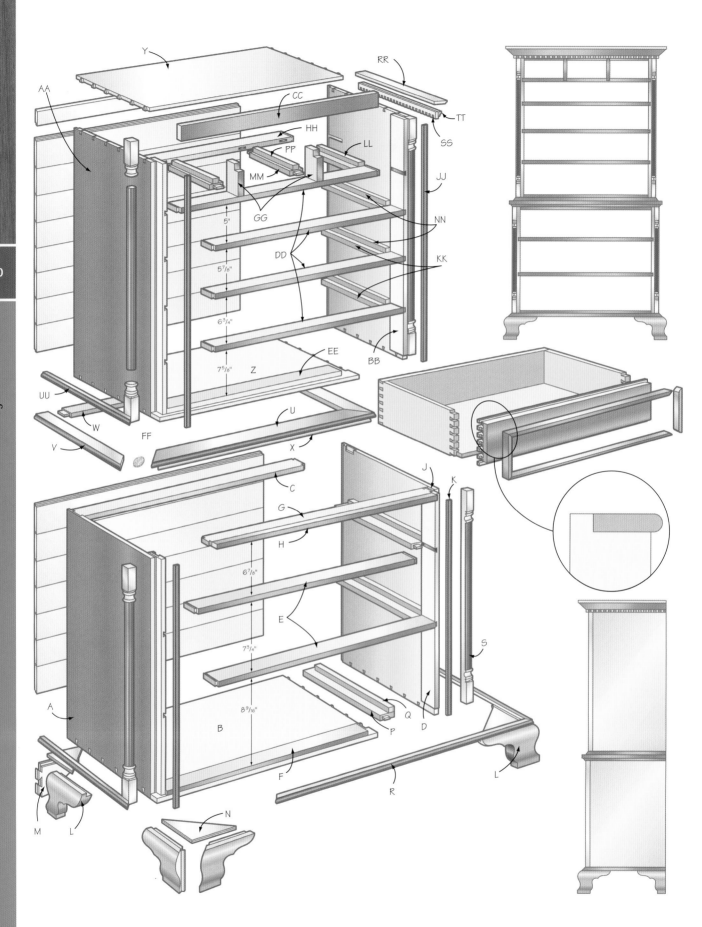

inches (millimeters)

REFERENCE	QUANTITY	PART	STOCK	THICKNESS	(mm)	WIDTH	(mm)	LENGTH	(mm)	COMMENTS
LOWER SECTION										
A	2	case sides	primary	3/4	(19)	19 5/8	(498)	28 3/16	(716)	
B	1	case bottom	secondary	5/8	(16)	20 3/4	(527)	37 1/4	(946)	
C	1	back brace	secondary	3/4	(19)	3	(76)	37 3/16	(945)	dovetail both ends
D	2	vertical case fronts	primary	7/8	(22)	5 1/2	(140)	27 9/16	(700)	two pieces at 2 1/2" (64mm)
E	2	middle dividers	primary	7/8	(22)	2 3/4	(70)	34 5/8	(879)	dovetail both ends
F	1	bottom divider	primary	3/4	(19)	2 3/4	(70)	33 3/8	(848)	
G	1	top divider	pri/sec	3/4	(19)	2	(51)	35 1/8	(892)	rear piece/dovetail both ends
H	1	top divider face	primary	3/4	(19)	1 9/16	(40)	33 3/8	(848)	
J	2	vertical front spacers	secondary	3/8	(10)	1 5/8	(41)	27 9/16	(700)	
K	2	vertical front faces	primary	1/4	(6)	7/8	(22)	27 9/16	(700)	
L	2	foot material	primary	1 1/2	(38)	5 9/16	(141)	31	(787)	8 7/8"-long (225mm) pieces
M	2	back feet	secondary	3/4	(19)	5 9/16	(141)	7 1/4	(184)	
N	4	feet assembly caps	secondary	1/2	(13)	6	(152)	12	(305)	triangular pieces
P	6	drawer runners	secondary	7/8	(22)	2 1/8	(54)	17 1/2	(445)	1/2" (13mm) tenon one end
Q	6	drawer guides	secondary	3/4	(19)	1 1/8	(29)	17	(432)	
R	1	base moulding	primary	7/8	(22)	2	(51)	45	(1143)	makes two pieces
S	4	quarter columns	primary	1 1/16	(27)	1 1/16	(27)	33	(838)	all columns
T	4	quarter columns	primary	1 3/16	(30)	1 3/16	(30)	12	(305)	all capitals
U	1	transition frame front	primary	7/8	(22)	3	(76)	39 1/4	(997)	
V	2	transition frame sides	primary	7/8	(22)	3	(76)	21 3/4	(553)	
W	1	transition frame rear	secondary	7/8	(22)	3	(76)	35 1/4	(895)	1" (25mm) tenon both ends
X	8lf	underhung moulding	primary	9/16	(14)	9/16	(14)			
UPPER SECTION										
Y	1	case top	pri/sec	3/4	(19)	19 7/8	(505)	35 5/8	(905)	
Z	1	case bottom	secondary	5/8	(16)	19 7/8	(505)	35 5/8	(905)	
AA	2	case sides	primary	3/4	(19)	18 3/4	(476)	37 1/8	(943)	
BB	1	vertical case fronts	primary	7/8	(22)	5 1/2	(140)	36	(914)	two pieces at 2 1/2" (64mm)
CC	1	case front top rail	primary	7/8	(22)	1 7/8	(48)	31 9/16	(802)	
DD	4	middle drawer dividers	primary	7/8	(22)	2 3/4	(70)	32 9/16	(827)	dovetail both ends
EE	1	bottom drawer divider	primary	7/8	(22)	2 3/4	(70)	31 9/16	(802)	
FF	2	vertical case front spacers	secondary	3/8	(10)	1 5/8	(41)	36	(914)	
GG	2	vertical drawer dividers	primary	7/8	(22)	1 5/8	(41)	5 7/16	(138)	
HH	1	rear drawer divider	secondary	7/8	(22)	2 5/8	(67)	34 1/4	(870)	
JJ	2	vertical front faces	primary	1/4	(6)	7/8	(22)	36	(914)	
KK	8	middle drawer runners	secondary	7/8	(22)	2 1/4	(57)	16 3/4	(426)	1/2" (13mm) tenon one end
LL	2	top exterior runners	secondary	7/8	(22)	2 1/4	(57)	15 3/16	(386)	1/2" (13mm) tenon one end, 1" (25mm) tenon both ends
MM	2	top interior runners	secondary	7/8	(22)	2 7/8	(73)	15 3/16	(386)	1/2" (13mm) tenon one end, 1" (25mm) tenon both ends
NN	10	outer drawer guides	secondary	5/8	(16)	1 1/8	(29)	15	(381)	
PP	2	interior drawer guides	secondary	5/8	(16)	7/8	(22)	15	(381)	
QQ	1	stage 1 cap moulding front	primary	3/4	(19)	3 1/2	(89)	39 5/8	(1007)	
RR	2	stage 1 cap moulding sides	primary	3/4	(19)	3 1/2	(89)	21 7/8	(556)	
SS	1	stage 2 dentil moulding	primary	3/4	(19)	1 3/4	(45)	48	(1219)	front and sides, 1/4" (6mm)
TT	2	stage 3 moulding	primary	7/8	(22)	1 1/4	(32)	48	(1219)	
UU	1	transition molding	primary	7/8	(22)	2	(51)	45	(1143)	front and sides

inches (millimeters)

REFERENCE	QUANTITY	PART	STOCK	THICKNESS	(mm)	WIDTH	(mm)	LENGTH	(mm)	COMMENTS
DRAWER PARTS										
VV	3	fronts #1-3	primary	$7/8$	(22)	$4^3/8$	(112)	$9^7/8$	(251)	
WW	1	front #4	primary	$7/8$	(22)	5	(127)	$31^9/16$	(801)	
XX	1	front #5	primary	$7/8$	(22)	$5^7/8$	(149)	$31^9/16$	(801)	
YY	1	front #6	primary	$7/8$	(22)	$6^3/4$	(171)	$31^9/16$	(801)	
ZZ	1	front #7	primary	$7/8$	(22)	$7^5/8$	(194)	$31^9/16$	(801)	
AAA	1	front #8	primary	$7/8$	(22)	$6^7/8$	(174)	$33^5/16$	(846)	
BBB	1	front #9	primary	$7/8$	(22)	$7^3/4$	(197)	$33^5/16$	(846)	
CCC	1	front #10	primary	$7/8$	(22)	$8^9/16$	(217)	$33^5/16$	(846)	
DDD	6	sides #1-3	secondary	$1/2$	(13)	$4^3/8$	(112)	$16^1/2$	(419)	
EEE	2	sides #4	secondary	$1/2$	(13)	5	(127)	$16^1/2$	(419)	
FFF	2	sides #5	secondary	$1/2$	(13)	$5^7/8$	(149)	$16^1/2$	(419)	
GGG	2	sides #6	secondary	$1/2$	(13)	$6^3/4$	(171)	$16^1/2$	(419)	
HHH	2	sides #7	secondary	$1/2$	(13)	$7^5/8$	(194)	$16^1/2$	(419)	
JJJ	2	sides #8	secondary	$1/2$	(13)	$6^7/8$	(174)	$16^1/2$	(419)	
KKK	2	sides #9	secondary	$1/2$	(13)	$7^3/4$	(197)	$16^1/2$	(419)	
LLL	2	sides #10	secondary	$1/2$	(13)	$8^9/16$	(217)	$16^1/2$	(419)	
MMM	3	backs #1-3	secondary	$1/2$	(13)	$3^5/8$	(92)	$9^7/8$	(251)	
NNN	1	back #4	secondary	$1/2$	(13)	$4^1/4$	(108)	$31^9/16$	(801)	
PPP	1	back #5	secondary	$1/2$	(13)	$5^1/8$	(130)	$31^9/16$	(801)	
QQQ	1	back #6	secondary	$1/2$	(13)	6	(152)	$31^9/16$	(801)	
RRR	1	back #7	secondary	$1/2$	(13)	$6^7/8$	(174)	$31^9/16$	(801)	
SSS	1	back #8	secondary	$1/2$	(13)	$6^1/8$	(155)	$33^5/16$	(846)	
TTT	1	back #9	secondary	$1/2$	(13)	7	(178)	$33^5/16$	(846)	
UUU	1	back #10	secondary	$1/2$	(13)	$7^3/16$	(183)	$33^5/16$	(846)	
VVV	65lf	drawer edge beading	primary	$3/16$	(5)	$3/4$	(19)			
WWW	8	drawer bottoms	secondary	$5/8$	(16)	18	(457)	35	(889)	cut to fit drawers
XXX	1	top section case back	secondary	$5/8$	(16)	$36^5/8$	(930)	35	(889)	many pieces
YYY	1	bottom section case back	secondary	$5/8$	(16)	$36^3/4$	(933)	$28^3/16$	(716)	many pieces

HARDWARE & SUPPLIES

16 semi-bright finish drawer pulls, Horton Brass PC-81

8 semi-bright finish drawer escutcheons, Horton Brass PC-81ES

1 drawer lock, Horton Brass LK-4

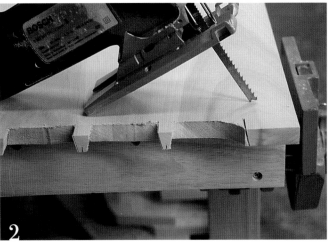

Starting with the lower section, mill and cut to size the case bottom and sides. Choose the best (face) side of the bottom panel. Layout the dovetail pins so that the tail's widest section is on the face edge. Make sure you have a 1¼" (32mm) half pin on the front edge at each end of this bottom panel.

Cut the lines that define the pins and remove the waste material. I like to use a jigsaw to remove the majority of the waste and then use chisels to clean up to the layout lines.

After scribing both sides with your marking gauge, select the face of the sides. Lay one side face down on the bench and align the back edge of the bottom with the side. Trace the pins of the case bottom to side. Remember that the bottom extends past the front edges of the sides. Remove the waste material to create the pins and fit the joints.

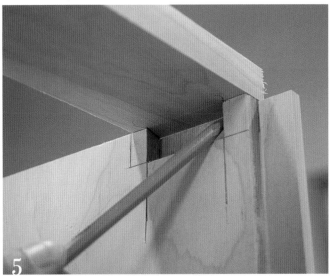

Cut a ¾" × ⁷⁄₁₆" (19mm × 11mm) rabbet into the back edge of each side. These rabbets will accept the backboards. Now cut a dovetail socket into the top edge of each side at the back. This socket will house the back brace. With the socket complete, glue and clamp the sides to the bottom. Be sure this assembly is square.

Mill the back brace to size and align its end with one of the case sides at the dovetail socket. Trace the outline of the socket onto the back brace. Cut the dovetails on the back brace and glue it into the sockets.

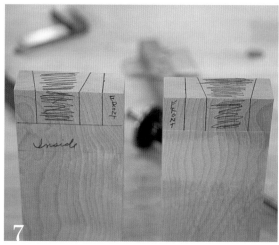

Cut the material for the vertical case fronts in one piece as shown in the cutting list. Lay out the locations of the drawer dividers on this piece. Use a router with a ¾" (19mm) guide bushing and a ¾" (19mm) dovetail bit. Use a straight-edge jig as a guide and route the groove for each divider. The bottom divider is cut to fit between the case sides — no dovetail!

Rip the vertical case front stock into two pieces that are 2½" (64mm) wide. Make a mark ½" (13mm) in from each front edge. Lay out a dovetail socket in the center of the remaining area. Remove the bulk of the waste using a band saw and clean up using chisels.

Cut out the vertical front spacers. Lay the case on its side and use glue and a couple of brads to attach the vertical spacers flush with the front edges of the sides.

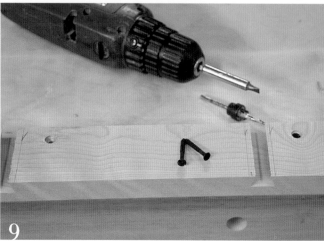

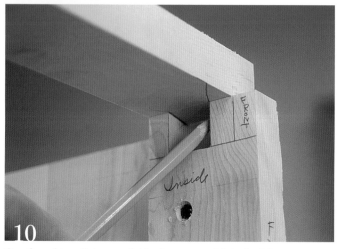

Make sure that the rear edge of the vertical case fronts are flush with the rear edge of the spacers, drill and countersink pilot holes and use No.8 × 1¼" (32mm) flat-head wood screws to attach the case fronts to the spacers.

Cut, fit and install the top divider just as you did the back brace.

Cut, glue and clamp the top divider face to the top divider as shown. Note that the the spacer is proud of the vertical front by exactly ¼" (6mm).

Prepare the stock for the drawer dividers. Run an additional scrap piece to the same dimensions. Each end of the middle dividers will receive a dovetail. Using the same dovetail bit that was used to cut the slots in the vertical fronts, first set the height of the cut and then the thickness of the dovetail. Use the scrap piece to be sure the setting are correct, then run the dividers. I like to install a fence extension to help support the dividers. If you use this setup like I've shown, be sure to feed the part left to right past the cutter!

Test-fit each divider, including the bottom divider, into the case.

Cut the ¼"-wide (6mm) by 1"-long (25mm) by ½"-deep (13mm) mortises into the back edges of the dividers at each end just inside the dovetail. The step method of mortising (cut a ¼" [6mm] hole, skip a ¼" [6mm] and cut another hole, then come back and remove the balance of the waste) helps to retain the sharpness of the chisel and bit.

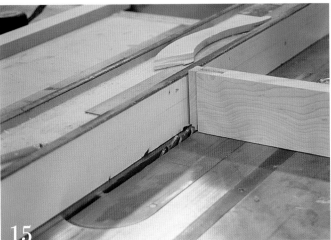

The middle dividers need one additional step before they can be installed. Set the table saw blade to ¼" (6mm) and remove the front of each dovetail. This is done to allow the vertical front faces to be installed.

Cut, mill, glue and clamp the vertical front faces in place. These pieces hide the dovetails and are found on many early pieces. These vertical faces should be flush with the front edges of the bottom, bottom spacer and top spacer.

16
Using glue and No.8 × 1¼" (32mm) flat-head wood screws, install the bottom divider flush with the front edge of the case bottom. Next, install the middle dividers with the face of the notch flush with the

17

tip

If you move hastily, as I did, and forget to notch the dovetail ends of the middle dividers, set up a straight edge along with a pattern bit and carefully remove the material flush with the vertical case fronts.

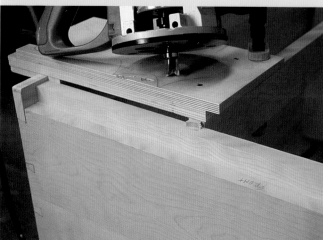

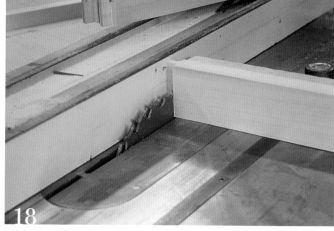

18
Mill and cut the runners to size. To create the tenon, make the shoulder cut first. Then make the cheek cuts that define the ¼"-wide (6mm) tenon. This tenon is offset 1⅛" (29mm) to reach around the fluted column area. The resulting tenon matches the mortises created in step 14. See the illustration for orientation of these parts.

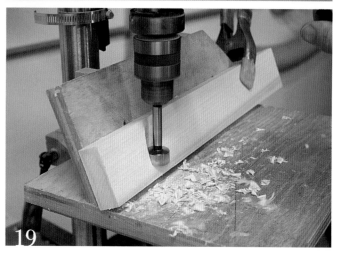

19
Tilt the runner stock 10° and use a Forstner bit to drill a pocket hole to accommodate a No.8 × 1¼" (32mm) flat-head wood screw. Double-check the depth of the hole to be sure the screw won't go completely through the side of the cabinet. Use a ³⁄₁₆" (5mm) drill bit to finish the hole.

20 Locate the position of the runners square to the faces of the drawer dividers. Don't use glue on the sides of the runners. The screws will hold them in place. Install the drawer guides using glue and brads.

21 Mill the stock for the quartered columns. Spread glue onto one of the pieces and apply a strip of brown paper bag. Now apply glue to this paper bag strip as well as the second piece of stock and clamp these two parts together. Glue up another set. When the glue is dry, mill one side smooth. Glue these two assemblies together with the brown paper bag between them. Glue up the material for the column capitals the same way.

22 Turn the column capital stock to profile according to the plan. Turn the profile on both ends of this stock. Next, turn the quartered column stock to the point of a smooth round and stop.

23 To divide the piece into eight equal sections, use a strip of paper. Wrap it around the turning covering only a quarter of the column (you should see the joint lines). Divide that into three sections with two full sections at the middle and two half sections at each end, as shown. These lines represent where you are to make the flutes.

24 To create the flutes, I've built a jig that holds my trim router which has a fluting bit installed (Lee Valley No.16j41.02). Align the center of the bit with the mark from the previous step, hold the stock to keep it from rotating and make a pass with the bit bearing running against the stock. Rotate the stock to center the bit with the next mark and repeat the steps until all the flutes, three per quartered column, are made.

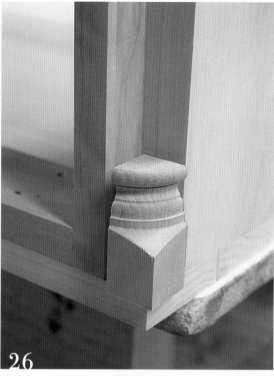

Trim one of the split capitals so that the flat or unturned section is 1⅞"-long (48mm). Be sure the capital is flush with both mating surfaces. Use glue and small brads to attach the capital. Repeat the steps for the top capitals. These need to be 1⁹⁄₁₆"-long (40mm) from the turned area. Fit these into position but do not attach. Make a mark at the end of the top capital. Measure from the top of the bottom capital to this mark. Cut the fluted column to this measurement. Double check the fit of the column with the top capital in place. Using glue and brads, install the fluted column and the top capital.

With the flutes made and the profiles turned, split the columns at the paper bag area. They should separate without a problem.

Make the base moulding by profiling two sides of the stock and ripping the piece into two pieces that are ¾" × ⅞" (19mm × 22mm). The base moulding is glued and nailed to the bottom edge of the case. Apply glue to the front piece and to the first 5" (127mm) of the moulding on each side. This is done to hold everything tight at the front of the case and to force the wood movement to the rear of the case.

Let's begin the feet! To start, mill the stock to size according to the cut sheet and trace the foot profile on the ends of the pieces, making sure to keep them aligned. Set the blade height to the top edge of the cove of the foot and put an auxiliary fence on the saw. Set one piece stock on each side of the blade and twist the fence until the point of the blade matches the end point of the cove of the foot just as it passes above and below the table top. At that position lock the fence in place. Lower the blade and gradually cut the cove in incremental steps until the full cove has been cut.

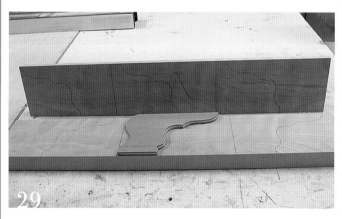

Next, use a pattern of the foot to lay out the individual feet. You will need three profiles facing in both directions. Place the pattern onto the stock, making sure the top of the pattern is at the top edge of the stock. Trace the profile onto the stock, then chop the stock into three pieces each 8⅞"-long (225mm) as measured from the tip of the foot. Cut the back profile of the foot using a band saw.

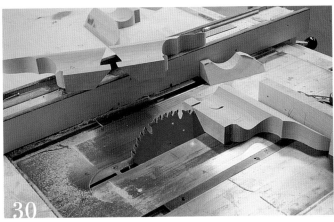

Tilt the table saw blade to 45° and cut the front edge of the foot, leaving approximately 3¾" (95mm) of material where the foot meets the floor. Choose the four blanks that look the best, two left-facing and two right-facing. These will become the front feet after they are paired. In this procedure, the two left-facing feet can be cut with the miter gauge in the traditional position. In order to cut the remaining feet you will need to reverse the gauge in the saw slot. In essence, you push the blanks through the cut while holding them against the miter gauge.

Before changing the blade angle, reset the fence to begin a ¼"-wide (6mm) groove for the spline in each of the four pieces. After two passes at the blade, each foot should have a ¼"-wide (6mm) by ⅜"-deep (10mm) groove for the spline.

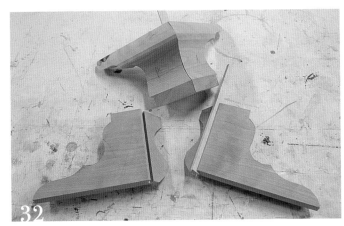

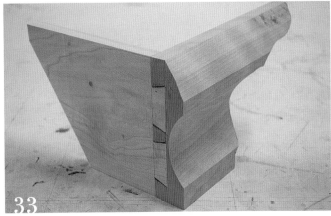

Cut a spline of plywood, apply glue and assemble two pairs of feet — one for each front corner of the chest.

Cut the remaining feet square, leaving 3¾" (95mm) of material at the floor, like you did in step 30. Then dovetail to the back feet as shown.

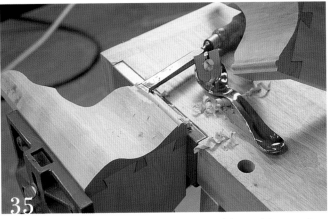

Cut a ¼" (6mm) bead at the bottom of each of the profiled feet. This will give you a "platform" foot versus a standard ogee bracket foot.

Complete the profile on the feet. The majority of the work is around the bead and the gentle rounding at the cove. The profile should be smooth to the touch. I find using a variety of chisels and a carver's spoon plane helpful for finishing the shaping.

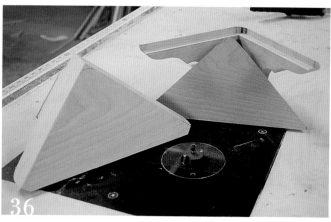

36 Use a rabbeting bit in the router table to form a lip that will allow the attachment of the feet assembly caps. Use glue and small brads to install the feet assembly caps.

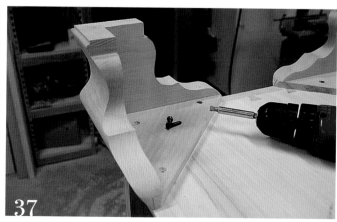

37 Attach the foot assemblies to the case using glue and screws. Align each foot with the base moulding for a smooth transition. Add glue blocks on the inside of each assembly to reinforce the foot — one in the corner and one out each wing.

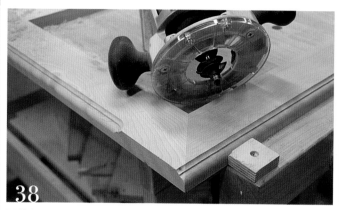

38 Mill the pieces for the transition frame to size and assemble the frame. See Massachusetts High Chest, steps 29-31 for assembly instructions.

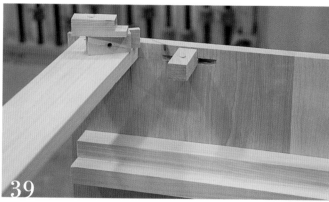

39 Attach the frame to the lower section using wooden clips. (See sidebar "Wooden Clips" following this project.) Mill a ¼"-wide (6mm) slot that begins ½" (13mm) down from the top of the sides. Using a biscuit joiner, make the first cut, then drop the cutter ⅛" and make the second. With the clips and slots cut, invert the chest onto the frame and install the clips using No.8 × 1¼" (32mm) flat-head wood screws. To complete the lower section, add the underhung molding below the frame. Install the moulding using small brads.

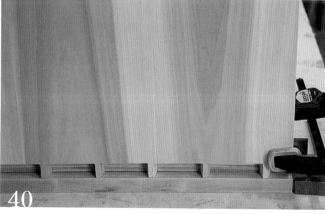

40 The construction of the upper section is the same as that of the lower section except that, along with dovetailing the case bottom you will dovetail a case top, as well. Form the pins in the case top and bottom as you did in steps 1-3. Mill the upper case sides to size and transfer the layout to the sides, remembering to hold the back edges even as in step 3. Complete the joint, trimming where necessary to get an exact fit.

41 Before you assemble the four pieces of the upper section case, remove ¾" (19mm) at the back edge of the case bottom. This will allow the backboards to extend down to the transition frame. Also, remember to cut the rabbets in the case sides to house those backboards!

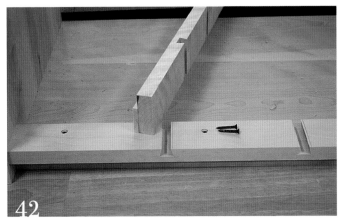

42

Next, create and install the vertical case fronts and case front spacers as you did in steps 6-9. Be careful with the layout of the drawer dividers. It works best if you do the layout beginning at the bottom and working to the top. Any adjustment for size can be made in the case front top rail.

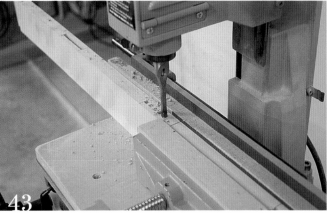

43

Mill all the drawer dividers to size, and create the dovetail ends on the front pieces. Cut the rear drawer divider square. Each drawer divider has the mortises for the drawer runners; however, the top divider and rear divider also need mortises that will catch the top interior runners. These mortises are ¼" (6mm) wide × 2⅞" (73mm) long × ½" (13mm) deep. Use the mortising machine for this operation.

44

Install the case front top rail with screws. Align it with the front edge of the case top and attach it through the case top and through the vertical case fronts. Remember that ¼" (6mm) offset that is shown? (See step 11.)

45

Install the drawer dividers by starting at the top. After the first middle divider is in place, cut and fit the vertical drawer dividers. Attach them using No.8 × 1¼" (32mm) flat-head wood screws. Put one screw through the middle drawer divider (remember that there is a mortise in this location), and run a second screw through the vertical divider and into the case front top rail.

46

Install the remaining middle and bottom front drawer dividers.

47

To install the rear drawer divider, use a carpenter's square set against the uppermost middle drawer divider to find the location of the rail. Use either the top edge of the front divider or the bottom edge. Use a straight-edge jig with a ¾" (19mm) pattern bit to plow the area for the rear drawer divider. Do this on both cabinet sides.

48

49

The rear drawer divider is ⅞" (22mm) thick and the groove is ¾" (19mm) wide, so unless you have a ⅞" (22mm) pattern bit, you need to trim the rear drawer divider to fit accurately. This is where it is important to lay out from the same point when routing that groove. While the layout of the vertical drawer dividers is nearly symmetrical, it is important to trim the rear drawer divider on the same surface on either end.

Next up are the drawer runners. Mill the runners to size, and create the tenons. The runners for the top row of drawers have a tenon on both ends. Each of these tenons are different in length (see cutting list). The balance of the runners are the same as those in the lower section. (See steps 18-20.) Here you can see the first set is in place and has the top interior runners positioned. Install the remaining runners and attach them to the case sides with the flat-head wood screws.

50

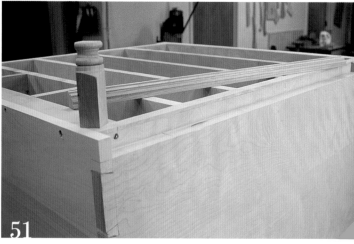

51

Install the vertical front faces to the upper section. A large number of spring clamps should make this job easier.

Split the second set of capitals and quartered columns for installation. Set the bottom capital so that there is 1¼" (32mm) length of square. The top capital has a square area that measures 2¼"-long (57mm). (See step 26.)

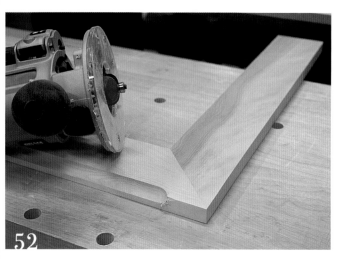

52

Begin the mouldings for the upper section by starting with the cap mouldings. Miter both ends of the front piece and one end of each side piece, then join them with biscuits and glue. Once dry, sand the unit and add the ½" (13mm) cove profile. In this step the mouldings are applied with No.8 × 1¼" (32mm) flat-head wood screws along the front and sides while gluing the front and only 4" (102mm) to 5" (127mm) along each side.

Next up is the dentil moulding. To make this moulding, set up the miter gauge and table saw with a ¼"-wide (6mm) blade, these are the blades for a dado set without the chippers. Raise the blade ¼" (6mm) and make a pass through the auxiliary fence attached to the miter gauge, creating a slot. Move the fence ½" (13mm) to the side, and fill the created slot with a piece of wood matching both the width and height of the slot. This will become the point to register the moulding with each cut. Start with the milled piece of stock against the filled slot, make another pass over the blade, then place the new slot over the point of register and make the next pass. The fit of the freshly cut slot must be fit snugly to the point of register to successfully make the dentil moulding. Once this is complete, slice the stock to the ¼" (6mm) width. This will result in two pieces of dentil moulding, enough to wrap the upper section just below the cap moulding.

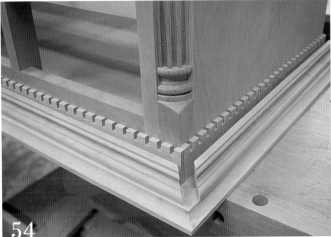

For the last step for the top mouldings, stage 3, use a classical router bit. I make it a practice to run a wide piece of stock through the bit at the router table and then rip the necessary pieces to size. After you attach the cap moulding, invert the upper section to make applying the mouldings easier.

The drawers for this piece are flush-fit drawers, meaning they are designed to sit inside the cabinet sides and drawer dividers — or flush with the front of the case. You need to fit the drawer fronts to the case, create the rest of the drawer parts from the sizes of the drawer fronts, then cut the dovetail joints in each drawer (see Massachusetts High Chest, steps 70-76). Next, cut the ¼" (6mm) groove in the drawer front and sides for the drawer bottoms, and glue the boxes (see Massachusetts High Chest, step 83).

The drawer edge beading will be applied in a rabbet that is cut in the drawer fronts. Place a straight bit in the router table and raise the height to ⅝" (16mm). Use an auxiliary fence, as shown, and carefully make a pass to create a 3⁄16"-deep (5mm) cut. Take a slow pass and run the box a couple of times if necessary. This step could also be completed using a rabbeting bit set to a 3⁄16" (5mm) cut. Make sure that the bearing is set appropriately.

Make the drawer edge beading by milling the stock to $\frac{3}{16}$" (5mm) thick × $\frac{3}{4}$" (19mm) wide and then passing it through a corner-beading bit. A $\frac{3}{16}$" (5mm) bit would be the first choice; however, a $\frac{1}{4}$" (6mm) bit can be used, but you will need to make a second pass to round both shoulders and sand the top profile smooth.

Cut the drawer edge beading, with mitered corners, to fit the drawers. Attach the drawer beading with glue and brads. Small amounts of glue are the answer; too much will squeeze out onto the drawer fronts.

Mill and cut the drawer bottoms to size, and attach them with glue and nails to the drawer boxes you assembled in step 55 (see Massachusetts High Chest, step 84).

The backboards can be made during the finishing process because they receive no finish. Mill the stock for the backs to $\frac{5}{8}$" (16mm) thick and create a half-lap joint on the edges of each board. Cut the individual pieces to fit the case, both upper and lower sections, and nail with an N-7 clout nail. Slightly angle the nail into the case side, but do not angle to such a degree that the nail penetrates the side!

To prepare the chest for finishing, sand the entire project with 180-grit sandpaper. I decided to stain the piece with a water-based aniline dye stain, equal parts of Moser's Golden Amber Maple and Brown Walnut. The staining process involves raising the grain of the piece with an application of water, sanding down the "fuzzies" with 320-grit sandpaper, flooding the stain on the project and allowing the stain to soak for about 10 minutes. Wipe away any excess stain. Next I sprayed two coats of Blonde Shellac, sanded and applied a coat of glaze. The glaze is sprayed onto the piece and allowed to start drying and then it is wiped away with soft a cloth. The glaze simulates years of aging because it remains in the crevices after wiping. After the glaze dried I sprayed on an additional three coats of shellac and then rubbed out the piece with No.0000 steel wool and Behlen's Wool Lube. I applied a couple of coats of paste wax to complete the finish.

WOODEN CLIPS

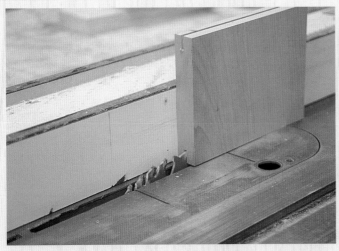

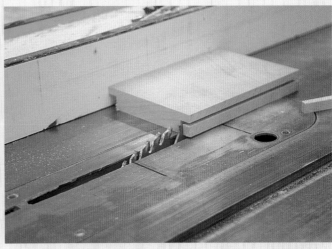

(STEP ONE) This setup works with a 1¼" (32mm) screw. Begin with a block of hardwood that is 4¼" (108mm) long and approximately 5" (127mm) wide × ¾" (19mm) thick. Set the fence at ¼" (6mm) and raise the blade height to ½" (13mm). Then, run the piece over the blade, cutting the end grain. Cut both ends.

(STEP TWO) Reposition the fence to remove the waste portion, creating a ½" × ½" (13mm × 13mm) rabbet. Again, cut both ends.

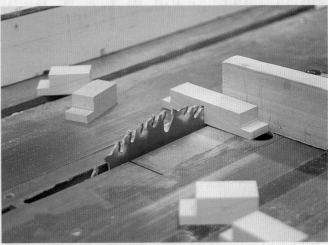

(STEP THREE) Set the fence at ⅞" (22mm) and rip the block into pieces. In a slot created by a biscuit jointer, ⅞" (22mm) works best .

(STEP FOUR) Using the miter gauge and a temporary fence, cut each ripped piece into two wooden clips.

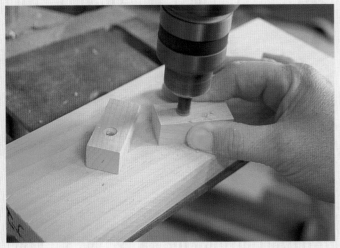

(STEP FIVE) Predrill and counterbore for a No.8 × 1¼" (32mm) wood screw, then slide the clip into the slot created in your project and install the screw.

PENNSYLVANIA
TALL CASE CLOCK

In the 18th century, tall case clocks were found in the most affluent homes, thus symbolizing the status one held in the community. A clock was often the most expensive furnishing in the home and was displayed where it could be admired by all who visited.

The clock movement was as important as the case, and during the mid to late 1700s brass was the movement of choice. To reinforce the owner's standing, the brass movement was also on display through the small window on the side of the clock's hood.

This tall case clock, based on a circa 1785 Philadelphia original, was selected by a customer to enhance a growing collection of handcrafted furniture. However, it may easily turn out to be the piece in his home that all visitors stop to admire.

Your tall case clock should have that same effect on your family and friends — and not just because you made it.

FROM THE COLLECTION OF MR. & MRS. BRAD KASPER,
COLUMBIA CROSS ROADS, PENNSYLVANIA

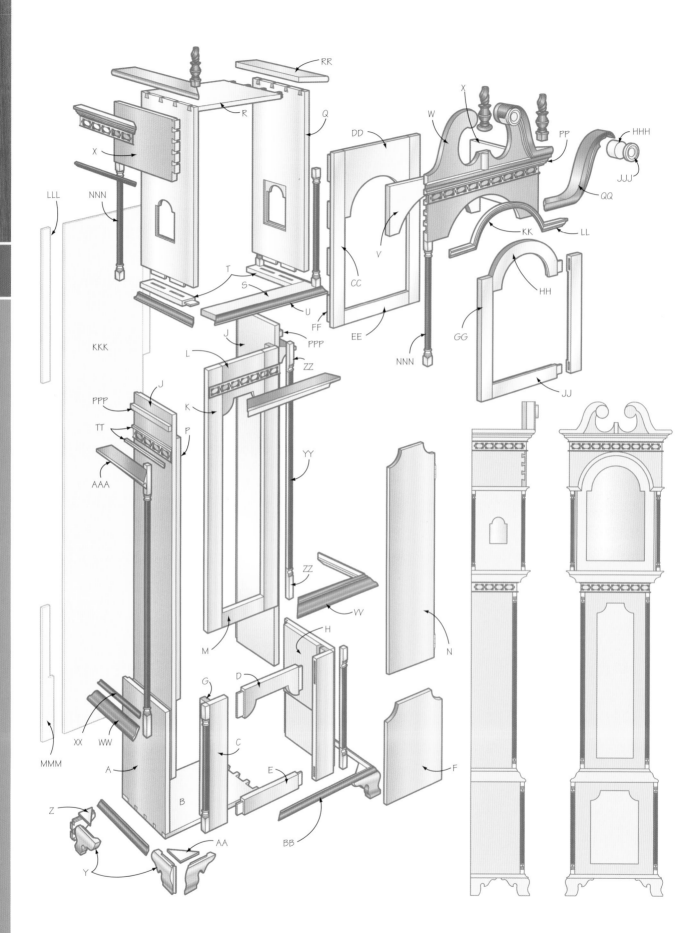

inches (millimeters)

REFERENCE	QUANTITY	PART	STOCK	THICKNESS	(mm)	WIDTH	(mm)	LENGTH	(mm)	COMMENTS
BASE										
A	2	base sides	primary	7/8	(22)	9 5/8	(245)	18 1/4	(464)	
B	1	base bottom	secondary	7/8	(22)	9 5/8	(245)	17	(432)	
C	2	base face frame stiles	primary	7/8	(22)	3 1/4	(83)	18 1/4	(464)	
D	1	base face frame top rail	primary	7/8	(22)	3 1/2	(89)	11 1/4	(286)	1 1/4" (32mm) tenon both ends
E	1	base face frame bottom rail	primary	7/8	(22)	2 7/8	(73)	11 1/4	(286)	1 1/4" (32mm) tenon both ends
F	1	base front panel	primary	3/4	(19)	9 3/8	(238)	13 3/4	(349)	
G	2	face frame connectors	secondary	7/8	(22)	1 5/8	(41)	17 3/8	(441)	
H	2	spacers	secondary	7/8	(22)	7 1/8	(181)	8	(203)	
WAIST										
J	2	waist sides	primary	7/8	(22)	7 7/8	(200)	53	(1346)	
K	2	waist face frame stiles	primary	7/8	(22)	2 1/2	(64)	40	(1016)	
L	1	waist face frame top rail	primary	7/8	(22)	7 1/2	(191)	9 1/4	(235)	
M	1	waist face frame bottom rail	primary	7/8	(22)	5	(127)	9 1/4	(235)	
N	1	waist door	primary	3/4	(19)	7 3/16	(183)	29 3/8	(746)	
P	2	face frame connectors	secondary	7/8	(22)	1 5/8	(41)	40	(1016)	
HOOD										
Q	2	hood sides	primary	3/4	(19)	9 5/8	(245)	25 3/8	(645)	
R	1	hood top	secondary	3/4	(19)	8 7/8	(225)	15 7/8	(403)	
S	1	hood bottom frame front	primary	5/8	(16)	1 3/4	(45)	17 1/8	(435)	
T	2	hood bottom frame sides	primary	5/8	(16)	1 3/4	(45)	9 3/4	(248)	1" (25mm) tenon one end
U	1	hood bottom frame moulding	primary	3/4	(19)	2 1/2	(64)	26	(660)	make a little more than 4' (1219mm)
V	1	pediment backer	primary	3/4	(19)	9 5/8	(245)	15 7/8	(403)	
W	1	scroll pediment	primary	7/8	(22)	16 1/8	(410)	18 1/8	(460)	
X	2	pediment returns	primary	1 1/8	(29)	9 5/8	(245)	10 3/8	(264)	
FEET										
Y	6	foot blocks	primary	1 1/2	(38)	3 3/8	(86)	5 5/8	(143)	
Z	2	rear feet	secondary	3/4	(19)	3 3/8	(86)	5 5/8	(143)	
AA	1	foot assembly cap	secondary	3/8	(10)	2 1/8	(54)	15	(381)	makes four caps
BB	2	base mouldings	primary	7/8	(22)	3/4	(19)	24	(610)	
DIAL FRAME										
CC	2	dial frame stiles	primary	1/2	(13)	1 1/2	(38)	21	(533)	
DD	1	dial frame top rail	primary	1/2	(13)	7 1/2	(191)	14 3/8	(365)	half-lap joint
EE	1	dial frame bottom rail	primary	1/2	(13)	2	(51)	14 3/8	(365)	half-lap joint
FF	8	dial frame glue blocks	secondary	5/16	(8)	5/16	(8)	2	(51)	
HOOD DOOR										
GG	2	door stiles	primary	3/4	(19)	1 7/8	(48)	18 3/16	(462)	
HH	1	door top rail	primary	3/4	(19)	6 3/4	(172)	13 5/8	(346)	1" (25mm) tenon both ends
JJ	1	door bottom rail	primary	3/4	(19)	2	(51)	13 5/8	(346)	1" (25mm) tenon both ends
BONNET MOULDINGS										
KK	1	front arched moulding	primary	5/8	(16)	7	(178)	17	(432)	
LL	1	front straight moulding	primary	5/8	(16)	4	(102)	12	(305)	makes three pieces
MM	3	small cove mouldings	primary	3/4	(19)	15/16	(24)	25	(635)	
NN	1	dentil moulding	primary	7/16	(11)	3	(76)	26	(660)	splits for two pieces
PP	2	topper mouldings	primary	5/16	(8)	1 1/2	(38)	26	(660)	makes three pieces

inches (millimeters)

REFERENCE	QUANTITY	PART	STOCK	THICKNESS	(mm)	WIDTH	(mm)	LENGTH	(mm)	COMMENTS
QQ	1	gooseneck	primary	$2^3/_8$	(60)	$9^1/_2$	(241)	$17^1/_2$	(445)	makes two pieces
RR	2	gooseneck side returns	primary	$3/_4$	(19)	$2^3/_8$	(60)	14	(356)	
SS	2	fretwork	primary	$3/_4$	(19)	$1^5/_8$	(41)	28	(711)	makes all pieces when split
TT	4	beading	primary	$1/_8$	(3)	$5/_{16}$	(8)	28	(711)	
UU	4	fluted columns	primary	$1^1/_{16}$	(27)	$1^1/_{16}$	(27)	$15^1/_4$	(387)	

WAIST MOULDINGS

REFERENCE	QUANTITY	PART	STOCK	THICKNESS	(mm)	WIDTH	(mm)	LENGTH	(mm)	COMMENTS
VV	1	stage 1 front	primary	$15/_{16}$	(24)	3	(76)	24	(610)	
WW	2	stage 1 sides	primary	$15/_{16}$	(24)	3	(76)	15	(381)	
XX	2	stage 2	primary	$9/_{16}$	(14)	$9/_{16}$	(14)	20	(508)	
YY	4	fluted quartered columns	primary	$13/_{16}$	(21)	$13/_{16}$	(21)	32	(813)	
ZZ	4	capitals	primary	$7/_8$	(22)	$7/_8$	(22)	12	(305)	
AAA	2	hood support mouldings	primary	$7/_8$	(22)	3	(76)	22	(559)	

FINIAL PARTS

REFERENCE	QUANTITY	PART	STOCK	THICKNESS	(mm)	WIDTH	(mm)	LENGTH	(mm)	COMMENTS
BBB	3	ball turnings	primary	2	(51)	2	(51)	4	(102)	
CCC	3	flame turnings	primary	$1^3/_8$	(35)	$1^3/_8$	(35)	5	(127)	
DDD	1	fluted block	primary	$1^1/_2$	(38)	$1^1/_2$	(38)	7	(178)	
EEE	2	block caps	primary	$1/_4$	(6)	2	(51)	2	(51)	
FFF	2	turned center columns	primary	$3/_4$	(19)	$1^1/_2$	(38)	4	(102)	need one half
GGG	1	turned center cap	primary	$1/_4$	(6)	2	(51)	2	(51)	
HHH	2	rosette fillers	primary	$1^3/_4$	(45)	$2^1/_2$	(64)	$2^1/_2$	(64)	
JJJ	2	carved rosettes	primary	$3/_4$	(19)	$2^7/_{16}$	(62)	$2^7/_{16}$	(62)	

BACKBOARDS

REFERENCE	QUANTITY	PART	STOCK	THICKNESS	(mm)	WIDTH	(mm)	LENGTH	(mm)	COMMENTS
KKK	1	main back	secondary	$5/_8$	(16)	$12^{13}/_{16}$	(325)	$80^1/_4$	(2038)	
LLL	2	hood back pieces	secondary	$5/_8$	(16)	$11/_{16}$	(18)	$19^5/_8$	(499)	
MMM	2	lower back pieces	secondary	$5/_8$	(16)	$1^{11}/_{16}$	(43)	$17^5/_8$	(448)	
NNN	4	fluted hood columns	primary	$1^1/_{16}$	(27)	$1^1/_{16}$	(27)	$15^3/_8$	(391)	
PPP	2	hood catches	pri/sec	$3/_8$	(10)	$5/_8$	(16)	$7^7/_8$	(200)	

HARDWARE & SUPPLIES

2 cupboard locks, Horton Brass LK-9

1 antique-finish large door escutcheon, Horton Brass H-67

1 antique-finish small door escutcheon, Horton Brass H-94

1 antique-finish hood door hinge, Horton Brass HDH-2

1 antique-finish waist door hinge, Horton Brass HDH-4

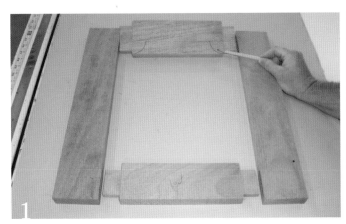

1

The face frames for the base and the waist both begin the same way. Cut the pieces to size according to the cutting list. Cut the mortises for the face frame rails into the face frame stiles. Cut a 1¼" (32mm) tenon at both ends of each face frame rail. Each of the two face frame top rails has a design cut into it. Draw a 1¼"-radius (32mm) quarter circle on the edges of each face frame rail, as shown; cut out everything below the pencil lines. Sand the edges, and assemble the face frames.

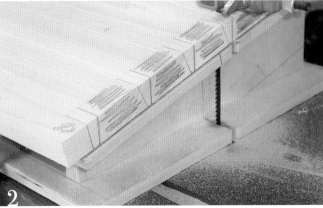

2

Mill the base sides and waist sides and the base bottom to size, and lay out the pins of the dovetail joint in the base bottom. Start the layout with a large half pin that will encompass a ¾" (19mm) backboard. With the layout set up in this manner the rabbet cut in the rear edge of the base sides will terminate on the base bottom. Make the angled cuts that define the pins, then remove the waste material with chisels.

3

Before you match the base bottom to the base sides to transfer the layout, make a two-step rabbet cut at the pin area. Do this so that the ¾" (19mm) moulding will cover the dovetail joint. Make the first cut with the piece flat on the table and the fence set at ¾" (19mm) (this added to the blade thickness [⅛" (3mm)] equals the thickness of the base sides). Make the second cut with the fence at ⅝" (16mm).

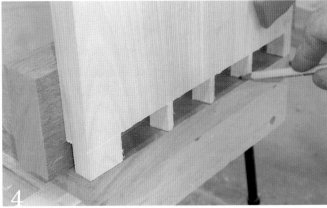

4

Set the marking gauge at ⅝" (16mm), and scribe a line on the two faces of the bottom edge of both base sides. Align the base bottom to the base sides and transfer the layout. Create the tails in the base sides and test the fit. Make any necessary adjustments.

5

Before you assemble the base bottom and base sides, make the rabbet in the base sides and waist sides for the backboards and make a rabbet along the back edge of the base bottom that is flush with the base sides' rabbets. The fit looks like this.

6

Sand the interior of the two face frames, and add the face frame connectors to the face frames. With both face frames the connectors are held flush at the top.

7

Attach the face frame assemblies to the base sides and the waist sides. For the base, the face frame sits on the base bottom, and the back edge of the face frame stiles fits even with the front edge of the base sides, producing a $\frac{7}{8}$" × $\frac{7}{8}$" (22mm × 22mm) area for the fluted quartered columns. The setup for the waist is the same except that it has no bottom.

8

Attach the face frame to the sides with screws installed through the face frame connectors.

9

Cut the parts for the feet according to the cutting list. Make 45° miter cuts and attach the four front foot blocks with a spline. Attach the two side feet to the rear feet with dovetails. (See Pennsylvania Chest on Chest, steps 30-33.)

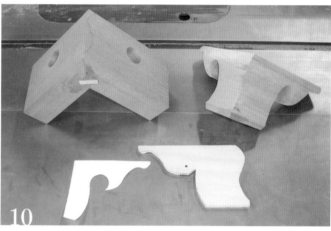

10

With the feet assembled, drill the holes and cut the design into the feet. For ease, drill the holes through the face of the feet; trace the design onto the inside of each foot and cut the design with a band saw.

11

Mark the foot profile onto the rear of the dovetailed foot assembly and onto one face of the mitered feet. Cut the profiles with a band saw, using a jig to hold the assembly off the table.

12

For the front foot assemblies, make one profile cut to the layout line, then establish the other cut line by using the exposed end grain of the opposite foot. Finish the profile by cutting to that line.

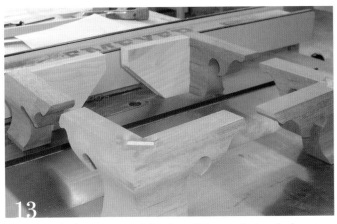

Shown are the four foot assemblies that will be attached to the base.

Use a rabbeting bit at a router table to make the cuts that will accept the foot assembly caps. Fit the foot assembly caps into the rabbets with glue and brads.

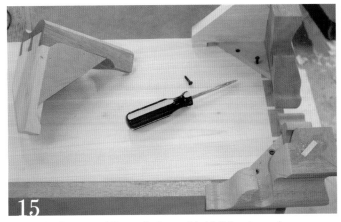

Attach the foot assemblies to the base with 1" (25mm) wood screws. Make sure that the assemblies extend beyond the edge of the base so that the base moulding, which will wrap the base just above the feet, will fit flush with the feet.

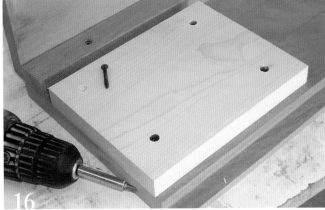

Install the spacers that allow you to attach the waist section to the base. Add glue to the pieces, and attach them using wood screws.

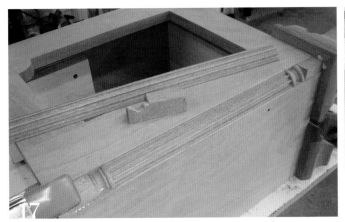

Make, cut and install the fluted quartered columns and the capitals into position on the base. (See Pennsylvania Chest on Chest, steps 21-27.) Of the four fluted pieces that you make in the process, one will be split to make the two columns in the base while two of the remaining three pieces will be used in the waist area. Turn the capitals so that you have two complete sets: a total of eight capitals when they are split. Four will be for the base, and four will be for the waist.

Make the base moulding, and apply it to the base just above the feet. Fit the mitered cuts at one front corner, then trim the side piece to length and attach the side piece. Next, cut the front piece to size and check the cut with the side piece held in position (shown here). If the cut is correct, attach the front piece, then finish by cutting the side length to size and installing the last piece. The router profile is a classic ogee bit.

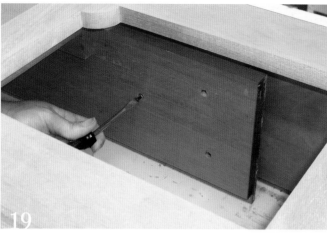

19

On a flat bench top or some other flat surface, fit the waist into the base and align the two sections into position. Attach the sections through the waist sides and into the spacers that you attached to the base sides in step 16. Hold the bottom edge of the waist face frame even with the top edge of the base.

20

Install the fluted quartered columns and capitals into the waist as shown. You can see the layout for the mouldings at the waist. Leave 1" (25mm) of the square portion of the capitals exposed above the mouldings.

21

Install the capitals at the top of the waist section; set the square area even with the flat section of the face frame top rail. Extend the square portion completely to the top edge of the face frame. (I had to add a piece to extend the square portion because I found that it was exposed under the fretwork!)

22

Begin making the hood support moulding by laying out the profile onto the ends of the two needed boards. It is important to do this layout as if you have one continuous piece divided in half. Do not turn the profiles! Adjust the auxiliary fence so that the blade tip enters the pattern as it appears above the table, as shown, and exits the pattern as it disappears below the table surface on the edge not shown.

23

Once the fence is adjusted properly attach it in place. Lower the blade and take a small pass cutting the roundness of the profile a little at a time. If you take too much of a cut the piece will become hard to push. Continue raising the blade in small increments until you have cut the profile.

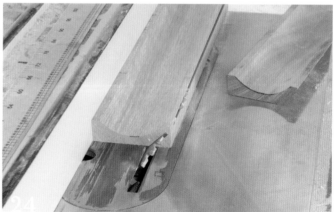

24

Set the blade to 45° and make the first two cuts, one on each side. You may need to slightly readjust the fence to make the second cut.

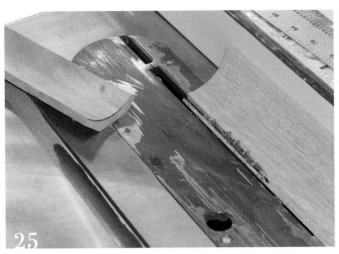

25

Set the blade to 90°. Cut the mouldings to have one leg at 2⅛" (54mm) and the second leg at 1½" (38mm), then sand them.

26

Install the hood support mouldings to the waist with glue and brads along the front edge; use just glue for the first few inches at the sides, and use brads to complete. Install each hood support moulding so that its top edge is ⅝" (16mm) below the top edge of the waist face frame top rail.

27

Begin work on the hood by milling the hood sides and hood top to size. Create the pins in the hood top, and set up to cut the matching tails in the hood sides. Set the hood top even at the rear of the hood sides, transfer the layout onto the hood sides, and cut the waste area for the dovetail joint.

28

Lay out the location of the arched top window in each hood side; the window should be 6⅝" (168mm) from the bottom edge of the hood side. Make a plywood pattern of the window opening, clamp the pattern in place, and use a router with a pattern bit to create the opening. Cut completely through from the face of each hood side. Finish squaring the windows' corners by using the pattern as a guide. The pattern is 3⅜" (86mm) wide × 5" (127mm) tall, and the radius of the arched top is 1¼" (32mm).

29

Before flipping the hood sides over to work on the interior, run the 3⁄16" (5mm) beading bit around the opening. Place on the interior of each hood side a pattern that is 4⅛" (105mm) wide × 7⅛" (181mm) tall over the opening with the window centered; rout the area for the glass. Make the arched area squared to accept the glass.

Finish the beading with handwork at the corners.

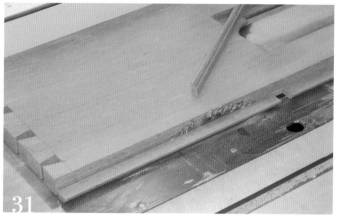

Run the ³⁄₁₆" (5mm) beading bit along the front outer edges of the hood sides. Make a two-step rabbet cut (⁷⁄₁₆" [11mm] wide × ³⁄₄" [19mm] deep) on the same edges, leaving the beading. Remove the beading in the area that is to accept the pediment backer, 9⁵⁄₈" (245mm) down from the top edge. While the blade is set for the second step in the rabbet, space the fence appropriately and make a few crosscuts at 9⁵⁄₈" (245mm). Reset the saw to make the cut removing the beading, as shown.

Mill the pieces for the hood bottom frame, create the mortise-and-tenon joints at the front, and lay out the mortises that will accept the hood side tenons. The layout is based on the width of the hood. The measurement of the area that is located inside the hood sides' inside edges, should be ³⁄₈" (10mm). Space the openings as shown, leaving enough material for solid support.

Start making the hood bottom frame moulding by running what is to become the top edge with a Roman ogee bit, as shown. Don't use the setup shown above. Bury the bit in a sacrificial fence and run the material against the fence and bit.

Create the ⁵⁄₈" (16mm) tenon on the bottom end of each hood side. Match the hood sides with the hood bottom frame sides to transfer the layout onto the tenons. Remove the waste material, and test the fit. If the fit is too tight you run a chance of splitting the hood bottom frame pieces. If it is too loose the fit will be sloppy. With the joint ready, glue the hood bottom frame sides into the hood bottom frame front and allow the glue to dry.

35

Using a classical ogee bit, run the bottom front edge of the hood bottom frame moulding. Don't use the setup shown above. Bury the bit in the sacrificial fence and run the material against the fence and bit.

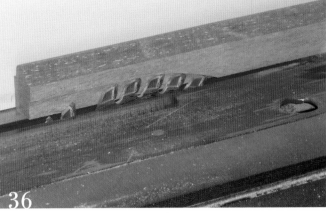

36

Cut the pieces to width and create a ¹⁄₈" (3mm) rabbet at the rear of the bottom edge of the hood bottom frame moulding. The cut depth should be deep enough so that, when attached to the hood bottom frame, the hood bottom frame moulding will slip over the hood support mouldings.

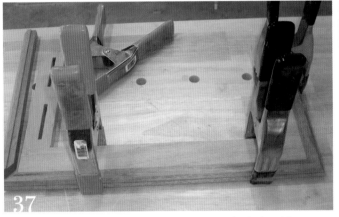

37

Miter the hood bottom frame moulding pieces to fit the hood bottom frame. Attach them with glue and spring clamps, as shown. Make sure that the rabbet orientation is correct.

38

Do some assembly. Apply glue to the pins of the hood top and slip the sides in place. Slide the hood bottom frame into position, but do not glue it. Place the clamps and check for square: Equal cross measurements mean that the unit is square.

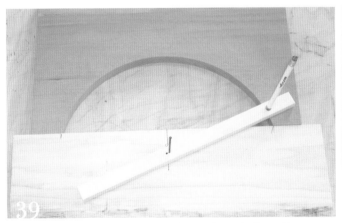

39

Mill the pediment backer to size and lay out the arched cut. Center the cut and make it 6¹¹⁄₁₆" (170mm) in diameter. Start the diameter at 1¾" (45mm) from the bottom edge of the piece.

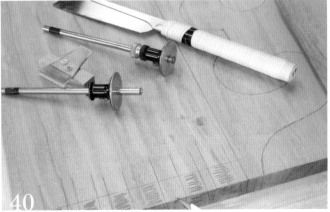

40

Mill the scroll pediment to size, and begin the layout of the joinery for the piece. Establish the "broken arch" areas, and lay out the area for the pins that will accept the dovetails from the pediment returns. Notice the slight variation in the dovetail layout. The extra spacing will keep the exposed dovetails aesthetically pleasing. The area to the right of the spacing will be covered with mouldings. The area to the left will then look balanced.

Hog out the waste material with a Forstner bit, staying inside the layout lines and cutting to the bottom of the joint.

Using your chisels, finish making the pins.

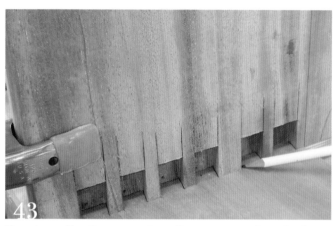

Place the scroll pediment onto the pediment returns and transfer the layout of the dovetails. Because of the size of the scroll pediment, I found it best to attach the piece to some type of straight-edged fence. Use the marking gauge to scribe the pediment returns and remember to orient them correctly.

Complete the tails in the pediment returns, and test the fit. Make any necessary adjustments.

Fit the pediment backer into the pediment assembly while you have the joints together. Mark the arch of the pediment backer onto the scroll pediment, then rough out the design.

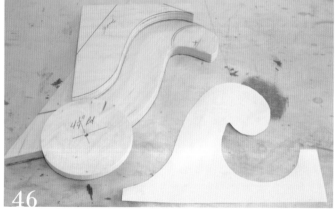

You can pull the layout for the goosenecks from the plans on the accompanying DVD; this is how I developed those plans. The bottom piece shown is the gooseneck as I would like it to be when cut. I place that gooseneck on top of a piece of plywood and use a 4½" (114mm) circle that I have turned with a lathe. The hole in the exact center of the circle allows for a pencil to draw a line parallel to the layout as the wheel moves along the profile. The radius of the circle is 2⅛" (54mm), which is the width of the gooseneck. Transfer the lines to cardboard to make a pattern.

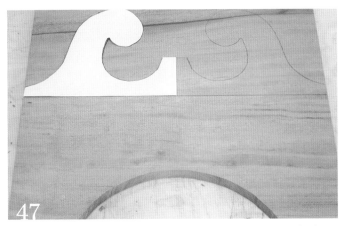

47

Lay out the gooseneck design onto the scroll pediment's front. The bottom edge of the pattern should be level with the top edge of the pediment returns. Cut the profile, and sand the piece smooth. I use a spindle sander with a variety of spindle sizes, and I also do some handwork.

48

Sand the inside of the pediment parts and assemble the dovetail joints with glue and clamps.

49

Position the pediment backer into the assembly, and attach to the pediment with glue and brads. To finish the pediment work, use a router with a pattern bit with a bottom-mounted bearing to trim the profile of the pediment backer into the scroll pediment. This will ensure an even pairing. Next, slip the unit over the hood assembly, and use screws through the hood sides to attach them.

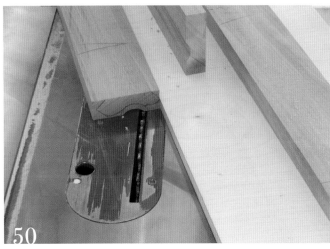

50

Make the stage 1 waist moulding next. Lay out the profiles, and cut the round at a table saw as you did for the hood support mouldings in steps 22-24.

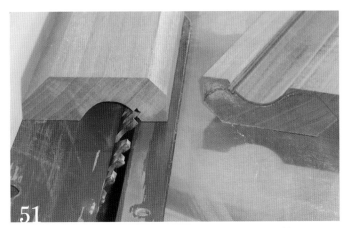

51

Set up to cut the groove that will give the stage 1 waist moulding a fillet near the bottom edge of the profile. Create this with the blade at a 45° angle.

52

Make the cuts the way you did in step 25. With the back of the stage 1 waist moulding against the fence, remove as much of the waste at the lower edge of the profile as possible.

To create the rounding detail at the lower edge of the stage 1 waist moulding, set the auxiliary fence in position so that a ¹/₂" (13mm) corner beading bit cuts with the top edge of the cutting surface just even with the lower edge of the fillet you created in step 51. Trim the bottom edge of the bead, and complete the profiling with planes, rasps and scrapers.

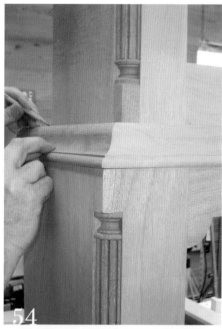

Cut the stage 1 waist moulding to fit the transition from the base to the waist. Use glue sparingly along the front and about 3" (76mm) down each side. Attach the stage 1 waist moulding with brads you drive through the lower edge of the molding into the top edge of the base and through the top edge of the stage 1 waist moulding into the waist.

Create, cut and fit the stage 2 waist moulding around the same transition and just on top of the stage 1 waist moulding. Use a classical ogee bit for the profile.

Set the parts together to get an idea as to how the clock is shaping up. Attach the base front panel using wooden clips screwed from the inside of the face frame (see Pennsylvania Chest on Chest, "Wooden Clips").

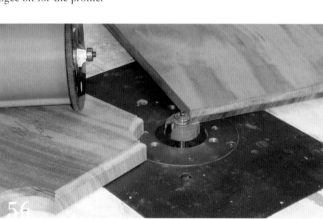

Cut the base front panel and the waist door to size. Draw the corner detail by laying out 1¹/₄"-radius (32mm) quarter circles like you did for the face frames in step 1. Cut that design into each piece. Run the ³/₁₆" (5mm) beading bit on the face side of each piece. Set up and cut a ³/₈" (10mm) rabbet on all sides of the base front panel and on three sides of the waist door. The only side that does not get a ³/₈" (10mm) rabbet is the hinge side of the waist door, there is a ¹/₈" (3mm) rabbet on that edge. You can cut this by changing the bearing on the rabbeting bit or by setting the table saw to make a matching cut.

To begin making the small cove moulding knock off one corner with the table saw blade set at 45°. Cut the cove portion as you did for the earlier coves in steps 22-23.

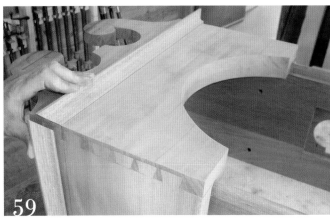

Cut the small mouldings and fit them to the hood. Attach the small cove mouldings with the ¾" (19mm) leg against the hood and set down ¾" (19mm) from the hood's top edge.

Mill the material for the dentil mouldings to size, run the coved edge with a router bit, and set up to cut the ⅛" (3mm) wide x ⅛" (3mm) deep teeth that are spaced ¼" (6mm). (See Pennsylvania Chest on Chest, step 53 for an explanation of making dentil mouldings.)

Create the topper mouldings, using the same router bit used in step 60 to make the cove. To prevent any glue from squeezing out into the profiled edges, put a small saw cut on the back side of the dentil moulding, as shown. This acts as a glue reservoir and catches any potential problems with the glue. Glue the dentil moulding to the topper mouldings. A few spring clamps should do the job. Allow the glue to dry.

When the assembly is dry, cut and fit the pieces to the hood. Add glue sparingly to the rear edges and attach to the small cove moulding. Run a few brads into the hood from the top side of the assembled moulding you made in step 61.

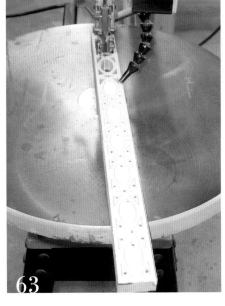

Print a few of the fretwork patterns and spray-glue them to the milled-to-size stock. Drill a small hole in each open area, and begin the scroll cutting to make the fretwork.

64

Use the fretwork in two places — just below the small cove moulding on the hood and just below the hood support moulding on the waist. In each place the design should be identical. Cut the beading to fit and attach. Use a pin nailer to attach the beading as well as the fretwork. Cut, fit and attach the fretwork; then finish with a second run of the beading.

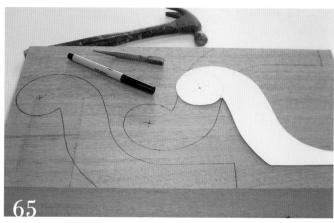

65

Make a pattern of the gooseneck from the hood, remembering that the long tail-like area is ³⁄₄" (19mm) thick to match the thickness of the moulding return pieces. If you choose to create the profile using a router, you will need to build a router jig as shown in "Making the Gooseneck" on page 91.

66

Cut and sand the gooseneck to size, then mount it onto a flat surface (I used a piece of melamine). With a ³⁄₄" (19mm) straight cut bit in the router, set the edge of the bit to cut ³⁄₄" (19mm) from the top edge of the stock. Position the guide arm (see photo step 67) to touch the stock and check the height of the flanges while the router is set in this position. Set the bit to a ½" (13mm) cut depth. Make a pass cutting the stock as shown, making sure to keep the arm against the stock and at a right angle to the line. Reset the router in position to remove the rest of the material without changing the cut depth.

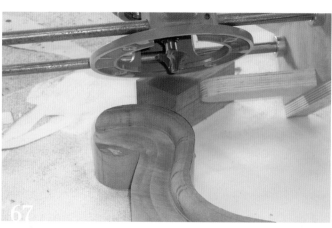

67

Use a ½" (13mm) ovolo bit or a modified cove bit. To use the cove bit, remove the bearing on a ½" (13mm) cove bit and make a pass to create the roundover effect shown. Use the guide arm and flanges as you did in step 66.

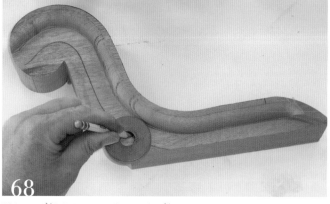

68

Using a 1³⁄₈" (35mm) washer with a ½" (13mm) center hole, mark the layout line for the next cut in the gooseneck. The flat shelf area that you see is where you will carve dentil moulding into the piece.

69

Use a ³⁄₄" (19mm) roundnose bit to cut to the line you established in step 68. Make this cut in a couple of passes, each time lowering the bit to end up with ⁷⁄₁₆" (11mm) of material at the bottom edge of the gooseneck.

70. Use a ½" (13mm) core box bit to create the last edge on the gooseneck. Here's a helpful hint: Use a marker to indicate the amount of bit that will need to be exposed to make the cut. Because of the depth of the gooseneck, the bit will be more exposed than it normally is.

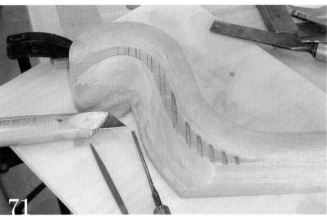

71. Carve the dentils into the gooseneck. The teeth are ¼" (6mm) wide and spaced at ⅛" (3mm) intervals. Note the variation in the length of the teeth.

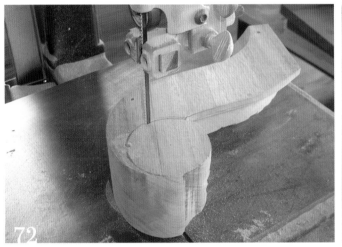

72. Lay out the rosette area, and cut away the waste with a band saw. Sand the area to the layout line using a spindle sander.

73. Position the gooseneck onto the hood and mark the point where you will cut the 45° angle. That is the point at the front corner where the front topper moulding and the side topper mouldings meet. Position a scrap piece of plywood that is cut on a 45° angle onto the gooseneck stock, and attach it with screws.

74. Make the 45° matching cut at a miter box, allowing the blade to align with the plywood scrap.

75. Attach the gooseneck to the hood, and repeat the steps for the opposite side. Then add the gooseneck side returns as shown.

Mill the pieces for the dial frame (the sizes depend on the clock dial and movement that you select). Cut half-lap joints for the door frame rails and door frame stiles. Make the cuts at a table saw and remove the waste with a straightedge and a router bit. Set the jig so that the rails extend from side to side. Then assemble the dial frame.

The completed dial frame should have a snug fit side to side and rest on the hood bottom frame. The dial frame should also be flush with the rabbet that is cut into the hood sides at the hood door area. To attach the dial frame to the hood use two screws at the top and small glue blocks along each side. Add some small brads to secure the glue blocks.

Begin the work on the hood door by milling the parts according to the cutting list. Lay out the door stiles for the door bottom rail, allowing a ³⁄₈" (10mm) shoulder on each edge of the door bottom rail. Move up the door stiles 11³⁄₈" (289mm) and lay out the door top rail. Even though this is a wide piece, only a small portion becomes the tenon. Before cutting the mortises, run the ¼" (6mm) beading bit along the inside edge of all the hood door pieces, set with a ¹⁄₁₆" (2mm) reveal.

Cut the tenons and set up for the 45° angle cut at the layout lines as shown. See the accompanying DVD for the steps to make this joint. Make the cut at the inside edge of each layout line on the door stiles as well as the shoulder layout of the tenons on the door rails. Draw a line that begins at the point of the angle cut.

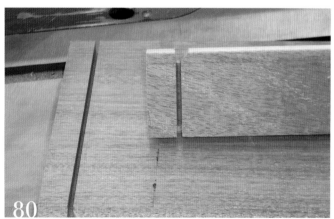

Use that line to set up the location of the shoulder cut that defines the tenons. Raise the blade to ¼" (6mm), set the fence so that the blade cuts on the waste side of those lines, and make the shoulder cuts on both ends of the two door rails. Raise the blade to ³⁄₈" (10mm) and make the shoulder cuts on the edges.

Use a tenoning fixture to complete the cuts on the door stiles. The cut should be even with the ¼" (6mm) beaded edge and extend up to the point of the 45° angle cut.

For the door top rail, cut the tenon to fit the mortise in the door stiles. Define the cut in from the end and remove the rest of the material with a chisel.

In order to have a space or rabbet for the door glass to fit into, you need to remove a portion of the interior edge of the door rails and stiles. Set up to make this cut at the ¼" (6mm) line and make the rabbet ⁷⁄₁₆" (11mm) deep.

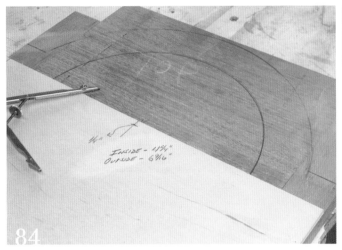

Assemble the hood door to check the fit in the hood cabinet. Then set a thin piece of plywood to just cover the ¼" (6mm) beaded detail and make the half circles for the door top rail. The inner radius is 4¾" (121mm), and the outer radius is 6 ⁹⁄₁₆" (167mm). Cut the inner half circle and sand the edge to a smooth finish.

At the router table, use a ¼" (6mm) beading bit to profile the front edge of the arched cut, as shown. Then, make a rabbet that will match up with those on the remaining pieces that comprise the hood door.

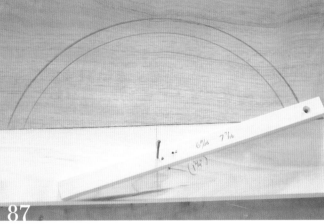

The next step is to assemble the hood door frame. Glue and clamp the pieces and allow it to dry. When dry, cut the outer profile and sand.

Mill lumber for the front arched moulding to size, and lay out the arch. Position a scrap board at the lower edge of the piece and move the pivot point for the arches down 1¾" (45mm) into the scrap. Draw the two radius lines, one at 6¹¹⁄₁₆" (170mm) and the second at 7⁷⁄₁₆" (189mm). Cut the inner radius and sand the edge.

88

Profile the edge of the front arched moulding with a classical router bit. With the same setup, cut the profile into the stock that will become the front straight mouldings. Cut the outer radius of the front arched moulding. Sand the cut smooth.

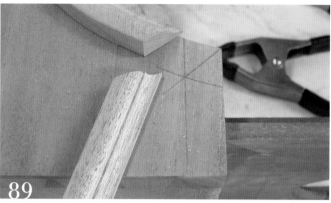

89

Cut and fit the front arched moulding miter. This will not be a 45° cut! To find the angle, place the front arched moulding onto the hood front in position with one edge extending off of the pediment. Draw a line, using the edge of the front arched moulding as a guide. Next, place a front straight moulding into position and trace the edge of that piece. Draw a line from the hood front corners to the intersection of the moulding lines, this is the angle needed. Cut the front mouldings to fit and install them with glue and brads. Be careful: The front arched moulding is fragile!

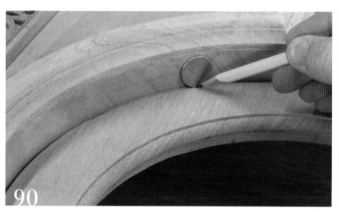

90

Place the hood door into the hood and check the fit. Look for a nickel's width gap in between the hood door and the arch of the hood. Make any necessary adjustments.

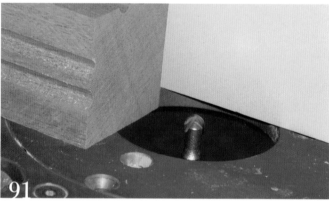

91

To make the fluted blocks that begin the finials, cut the blank to size and set up a ¼" (6mm) fluting bit at a router table. The fluted block gets four flutes per side on two adjacent sides. The flutes are equally spaced across the face of the block. Set up the cuts, run one cut, reverse the block, and run the second cut for the same face. Rotate the stock a quarter turn and repeat this on the second face. Then reset and cut two more flutes (for a total of four) on the two faces you just routed.

92

Position the fluted blocks half on the gooseneck side returns and half on the gooseneck. In order to have a level surface to attach the block, use chisels to flatten the slight rise in the gooseneck.

93

Make the block caps by milling two pieces of stock to the needed size and ¾" (19mm) thick. Use double-sided tape to affix the block caps to the bench, and run a ¼" (6mm) bead profile on all the edges. Slice the block caps to ¼" (6mm) thickness.

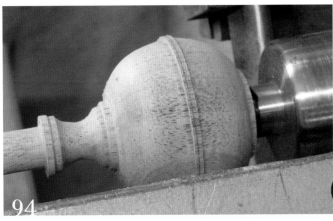

94

Turn the ball turnings to size according to the plans. At the same time, glue up the pieces that make up the turned center column. The two pieces get the brown paper bag between them, as you did with the fluted columns, so they can be split easily. Turn the short column to size.

95

Turn the flame turnings to size as well. The red line represents the widest point in the profile.

96

To lay out the carving for the flame turnings, start with a line that is shaped as shown and that represents a quarter turn around the piece.

97

Draw three lines around the flame turning to divide it into four sections, as shown. Around the base and top of the flame turning, divide it into six equal sections starting at the intersection of one dividing line and the shaped line from step 96. Around the two other dividing lines, equally space nine sections, again starting at the intersection.

The shaped line is the first of three lines in a set. There are three sets of lines on each flame turning. The second line, that to the right of the shaped line, begins at the base and stops before it reaches the top. The third line, again to the right of the previous line, begins at the top and stops before it reaches the bottom. Repeat this pattern around the flame turning.

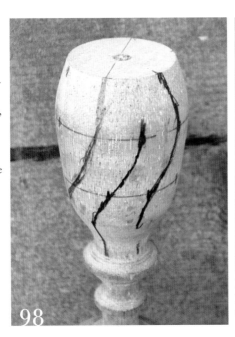

98

99

Begin the carving. While you can complete this with carving chisels, I like to use a flexible shaft power carver. The lines are the ridges of the carving, while the areas between the lines are the valleys.

100

To begin assembly of the finials, drill into the fluted blocks a ½" (13mm) hole that stops ⅝" (16mm) before the bottom edge of the fluted block. Drill a ½" (13mm) hole all the way through the block caps and about ⅝" (16mm) into the ball turnings. Attach the fluted columns to the hood with screws that go through the ½" (13mm) hole and get driven into the hood.

101

Split the turned center column from step 94 into two halves. Cut, fit, and glue one half onto the hood. Notice that I have added two slight grooves down either side of the turned center column. These act as glue reservoirs to prevent squeeze-out onto the pediment. Once the glue is dry, locate the center of the turned center column — that is the point where you will drill the hole to accept the finial.

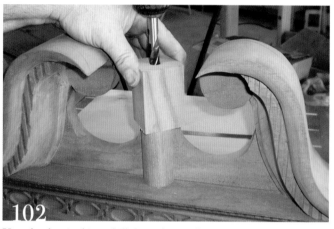

102

Use a brad-point bit to drill through a small scrap block. That block will be your guide to drill the hole for the finial. Set the point of the bit to your mark, hold the scrap block tightly against the turned center column and drill to the needed depth.

103

Make the turned center cap with a lathe. Drill the hole using the centering marks from the lathe mounting and install the turned center cap.

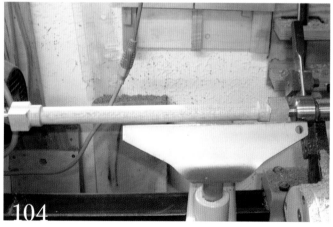

104

Turn the stock for the fluted hood columns to size, and profile the capitals in each piece.

105

Set up to flute the columns: First, build a plywood box that will hold the turnings level. Next, attach the column in that jig with screws from each end into the center of the turnings from the lathe mounting. Finally, chuck a ¼" (6mm) fluting bit into a router table.

106

Raise the bit so that it cuts into the fluted hood column about $^3/_{16}$"
(5mm), position the fence so that the bit is centered to the fluted
hood column, and set stops on the fence that will end the cuts about
$^1/_4$" (6mm) from the capital areas. Make eight flutes on each fluted
hood column. Place a mark for the center of the column on the jig
and extend the mark to the turning. Make four passes with that mark
in the center of one capital face. Make the other four passes with one
corner of the capital located at that mark. This setup is shown at the
beginning of one of the first four passes. Position the jig against the
stop, plunge down onto the bit, and run the cut to the second stop.

108

Add a $^3/_8$" (10mm) dowel as a tenon at the top end of
each fluted hood column. Using a $^3/_8$" (10mm) spade bit
with an extension, drill the hole for that tenon into the
undersides of the pediment returns, as shown. To find
the center point for the hole, draw a line on the square
end of the column connecting diagonal corners. Draw
another line connecting the other opposite corners.
Where the lines cross is the center of the column.

107

You can raise or lower the bit to get the correct setting. Make eight
cuts in each of the four fluted hood columns.

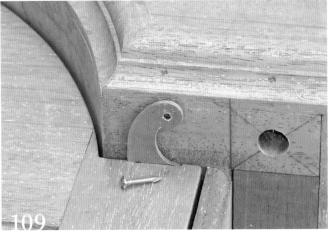

109

Install the specialty hinges for the clock. Attach the hinges to the top
and bottom of the right-hand door stile of the hood door. Turn the
curve of the hinge away from the door. Set the hinges into the door
half the thickness of the hinge plate. You may need to remove a little
material from the interior edge of the door stile for smooth door operation.

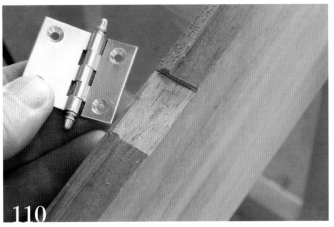

110

To hang the waist door, trim the $^1/_8$" (3mm) lip of the waist door to
allow the hinge to fit. The barrel of the hinge should fit snugly
against the $^3/_{16}$" (5mm) bead detail. Install the screws and position the
door into the opening. Transfer the layout of the hinges to the waist
front frame and remove the waste material. Attach the hinge leaf to
the case.

111

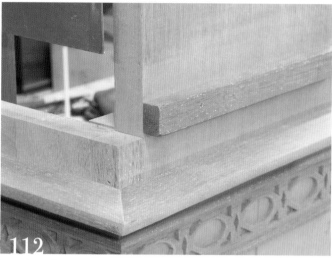

112

The rosette shown was made with a rosette cutter. (The actual rosette the customer selected is highly carved and beyond the scope of this book.) To install the rosette you must first install the rosette fillers. Glue them into the areas in the gooseneck mouldings. Glue the finished carved rosettes to the rosette fillers and into the goosenecks.

In order to keep the hood from tipping forward during the removal and installation process, add the hood catches to the waist sides just above the hood support moulding. Set these pieces high enough to not impair the sliding of the hood but tight enough to hold the hood in position.

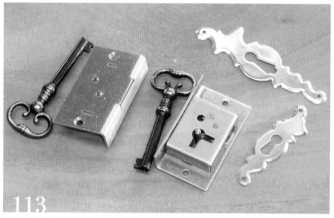

113

Fit the half-mortise locks to the hood door and the waist door. Attach the escutcheons after the finishing process. Also, because the clock needs to sit level in order for the movement to work accurately, you might want to install some type of adjustable leveler feet on the bottom of the clock case (not shown).

The back is installed after the clock has been stained and finished. The middle section of the back runs from top to bottom on the clock case while the two hood back pieces are the fillers for the step out of the hood. The lower back pieces are fillers for the base but also fit around the rabbeted area of the waist sides as they extend into the base. Glue these five back pieces together to create a one-piece back and attach it to the clock case with nails.

The clock is ready to finish after a final sanding. Do not attach the fluted hood columns before finishing. Once finishing steps are completed, install the glass in the hood door and in the hood windows. I used full restoration glass in the hood door and windows. Water putty keeps the glass in place. Install the fluted columns by using glue at the dowels and screws through the hood bottom frame.

114

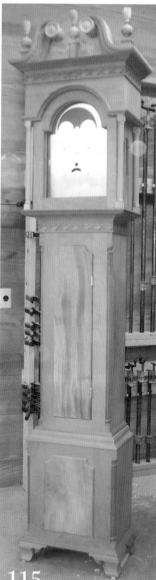

115

MAKING THE GOOSENECK

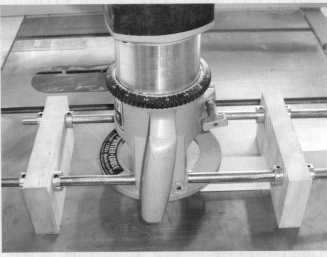

(STEP ONE) To make the router jig to cut the gooseneck, first determine the diameter of rod that will fit into your router's base. Set the router (without its plastic base) on a 2⅜" (60mm)-thick piece of stock to determine the necessary hole location for the rods. Set the end piece in place and mark each location with a brad-point bit that matches the diameter of the holes. Use a drill press to bore these holes.

(STEP TWO) Slide the rods through the router and the end pieces, and secure the rods with connectors. Space the end pieces about 15½" (394mm) apart.

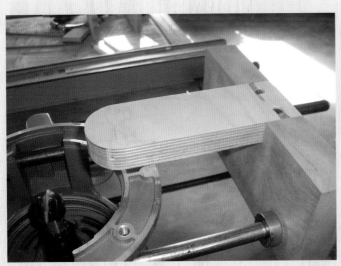

(STEP THREE) Notch the bottom edge of one end piece to install the guide arm. This piece is ¾"-thick (19mm) by 2"-wide (51mm) by 6"-long (152mm). The radius at the end is 1" (25mm). Fit the arm into the notched area, and secure it with screws. I added a ¾" (19mm) piece of plywood to the bottom edge of the end pieces to raise the router up higher. Now you are ready to install a router bit and begin shaping the goosenecks.

tip

With certain areas in my turnings along with any tenons I need, I like to use an open end wrench to adjust the cut to the correct size. Wrenches are "dead on" in sizing!

NEW ENGLAND DESK AND BOOKCASE

(SECRETARY)

Tiger maple was a favorite wood with cabinet-makers in New England during the 18th century. One of the most outstanding furniture selections from that time period is the secretary. Combining the two delivers a powerful statement!

When the patrons of this secretary first inquired about this piece, we had a version of the desk that delivered what they had envisioned. The bookcase was selected, and the interior was designed to fit their desires. The result was a great pairing of the two!

Secretaries can run from the sedate to the magnificent. This secretary is definitely reaching for the upper echelon with the cathedral interior that wraps around the desk as it steps back in layers and the fitted interior of the bookcase section, which also displays carved fans behind the tombstone doors.

FROM THE COLLECTION OF MR. & MRS. JAMES FAULKE,
NORTH WALES, PENNSYLVANIA

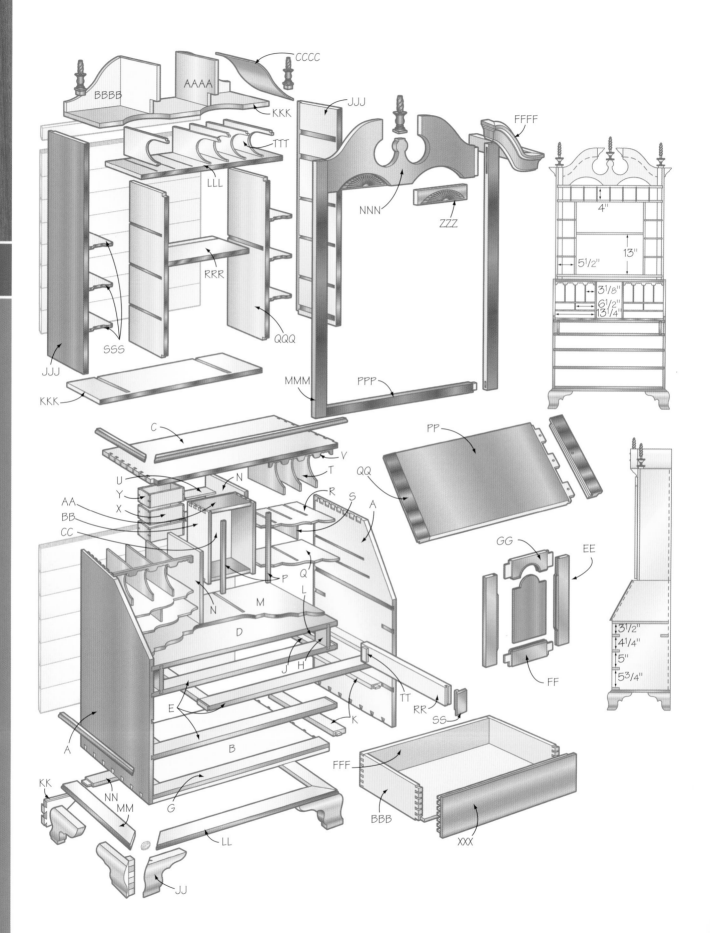

inches *(millimeters)*

REFERENCE	QUANTITY	PART	STOCK	THICKNESS	(mm)	WIDTH	(mm)	LENGTH	(mm)	COMMENTS
DESK SECTION										
A	2	case sides	primary	$3/4$	(19)	$19^1/_2$	(495)	$35^1/_2$	(902)	
B	1	case bottom	secondary	$3^5/_8$	(92)	$19^1/_2$	(495)	$37^1/_2$	(953)	
C	1	case top	primary	$3/4$	(19)	$12^3/_4$	(324)	37	(940)	
D	1	writing surface	primary	$3/4$	(19)	$18^3/_4$	(476)	$36^3/_8$	(924)	
E	3	drawer dividers	primary	$3/4$	(19)	$2^1/_2$	(64)	$36^7/_8$	(937)	dovetail ends
F	1	rear divider	secondary	$3/4$	(19)	$2^1/_2$	(64)	$36^7/_8$	(937)	dovetail end
G	1	bottom divider	primary	$3/4$	(19)	$2^1/_2$	(64)	$35^7/_8$	(911)	
H	2	vertical dividers	primary	$3/4$	(19)	$1^3/_4$	(45)	$4^3/_8$	(111)	lid supports
J	2	top drawer runners	secondary	$3/4$	(19)	$2^5/_8$	(67)	$15^1/_8$	(384)	$1/2$" (13mm) tenon one end, 1" (25mm) tenon one end
K	6	drawer runners	secondary	$3/4$	(19)	1	(25)	$16^5/_8$	(422)	$1/2$" (13mm) tenon one end
L	2	drawer guides	secondary	$3/4$	(19)	$3/4$	(19)	$15^1/_4$	(387)	top drawer
DESK INTERIOR										
M	1	interior base	primary	$9/16$	(14)	$14^3/_4$	(375)	36	(914)	
N	2	vertical dividers	primary	$1/2$	(13)	$10^1/_4$	(260)	$11^5/_8$	(295)	around box
P	2	vertical divider fronts	primary	$1/4$	(6)	$1/4$	(6)	$11^1/_8$	(283)	
Q	2	horizontal dividers (level 1)	primary	$3/8$	(10)	$13^1/_2$	(343)	$13^3/_4$	(349)	
R	2	horizontal dividers (level 2)	primary	$3/8$	(10)	$12^3/_4$	(324)	$13^3/_4$	(349)	
S	2	vertical dividers (level 2)	primary	$3/8$	(10)	$10^1/_4$	(260)	$2^1/_{16}$	(52)	
T	6	cubbyhole dividers	primary	$1/4$	(6)	$10^5/_8$	(270)	$6^7/_8$	(175)	
U	2	hidden drawer dividers	secondary	$1/4$	(6)	$3^1/_8$	(79)	$8^3/_4$	(222)	
V	2	valance material	primary	$1/4$	(6)	$1^1/_4$	(32)	16	(406)	eight pieces required
W	8	valance blocks	secondary	$5/16$	(8)	$5/16$	(8)	$2^3/_4$	(70)	
HIDDEN DRAWER BOXES										
X	6	fronts and backs	pri/sec	$3/8$	(10)	$3^1/_4$	(83)	$8^7/_{16}$	(214)	
Y	6	sides	pri/sec	$3/8$	(10)	$3^1/_4$	(83)	3	(76)	
Z	3	bottoms	pri/sec	$1/4$	(6)	3	(76)	$8^7/_{16}$	(214)	
PROSPECT DOOR BOX										
AA	2	top & bottom	primary	$1/2$	(13)	$5^1/_2$	(140)	$8^7/_{16}$	(214)	
BB	2	sides	primary	$1/2$	(13)	$6^1/_2$	(165)	$11^1/_8$	(282)	
CC	1	back	secondary	$1/4$	(6)	$7^7/_8$	(200)	$11^1/_8$	(282)	
DD	2	front face pieces	primary	$1/4$	(6)	$3/4$	(19)	$11^3/_{16}$	(284)	
PROSPECT DOOR										
EE	2	stiles	primary	$3/4$	(19)	$1^5/_8$	(41)	$11^1/_8$	(283)	
FF	1	lower rail	primary	$3/4$	(19)	$1^5/_8$	(41)	$6^1/_{16}$	(154)	1" (25mm) tenon both ends
GG	1	top rail	primary	$3/4$	(19)	$2^5/_8$	(67)	$6^1/_{16}$	(154)	1" (25mm) tenon both ends
HH	1	panel	primary	$1/4$	(6)	$4^{13}/_{16}$	(122)	$7^5/_8$	(194)	
JJ	2	foot blanks	primary	$1^5/_8$	(41)	$5^3/_4$	(146)	30	(762)	six pieces required
KK	2	rear feet	secondary	$3/4$	(19)	$5^3/_4$	(146)	7	(178)	
LL	1	base frame front	primary	$3/4$	(19)	$2^5/_8$	(67)	40	(1016)	angle cut both ends
MM	2	base frame sides	primary	$3/4$	(19)	$2^5/_8$	(67)	$20^5/_8$	(524)	angle cut one end
NN	1	base frame back	secondary	$3/4$	(19)	$2^5/_8$	(67)	$36^3/_4$	(934)	1" (25mm) tenon both ends
PP	1	desk lid	primary	$3/4$	(19)	14	(356)	$34^7/_8$	(886)	$1^1/_8$" (29mm) tenon both ends
QQ	2	breadboard ends	primary	$3/4$	(19)	2	(51)	15	(381)	
RR	2	lid supports	secondary	$13/16$	(21)	$3^7/_{16}$	(87)	$17^5/_8$	(448)	
SS	2	support faces	primary	$3/4$	(19)	$1^5/_8$	(41)	$3^1/_2$	(89)	
TT	2	support stops	secondary	$5/8$	(16)	$1^{11}/_{16}$	(43)	$2^3/_8$	(61)	

inches (millimeters)

REFERENCE	QUANTITY	PART	STOCK	THICKNESS	(mm)	WIDTH	(mm)	LENGTH	(mm)	COMMENTS
DRAWER PARTS										
UU	1	drawer front 1	primary	$3/4+$	(19)	$3^1/_2$	(89)	$33^1/_4$	(845)	
VV	1	drawer front 2	primary	$3/4+$	(19)	$4^1/_2$	(114)	$36^5/_8$	(930)	
WW	1	drawer front 3	primary	$3/4+$	(19)	$5^1/_4$	(133)	$36^5/_8$	(930)	
XX	1	drawer front 4	primary	$3/4+$	(19)	6	(152)	$36^5/_8$	(930)	
YY	2	drawer 1 sides	secondary	$1/2$	(13)	$3^7/_{16}$	(87)	16	(406)	
ZZ	2	drawer 2 sides	secondary	$1/2$	(13)	$4^1/_8$	(105)	16	(406)	
AAA	2	drawer 3 sides	secondary	$1/2$	(13)	$4^7/_8$	(124)	16	(406)	
BBB	2	drawer 4 sides	secondary	$1/2$	(13)	$5^5/_8$	(143)	16	(406)	
CCC	1	drawer 1 back	secondary	$1/2$	(13)	$2^{15}/_{16}$	(75)	$32^1/_2$	(826)	
DDD	1	drawer 2 back	secondary	$1/2$	(13)	$3^5/_8$	(92)	$35^{13}/_{16}$	(910)	
EEE	1	drawer 3 back	secondary	$1/2$	(13)	$4^3/_8$	(111)	$35^{13}/_{16}$	(910)	
FFF	1	drawer 4 back	secondary	$1/2$	(13)	$4^7/_8$	(124)	$35^{13}/_{16}$	(910)	
GGG	1	top drawer bottom	secondary	$5/8$	(16)	16	(406)	$32^1/_2$	(826)	
HHH	3	drawer bottoms	secondary	$5/8$	(16)	16	(406)	$35^3/_4$	(908)	cut to fit
BOOKCASE SECTION										
JJJ	2	case sides	primary	$3/4$	(19)	$10^1/_2$	(267)	$36^1/_8$	(918)	
KKK	2	case shelves, top and bottom	pri/sec	$3/4$	(19)	$9^3/_4$	(248)	35	(889)	
LLL	1	case middle shelf	pri/sec	$5/8$	(16)	$9^3/_4$	(248)	35	(889)	
MMM	2	face frame stiles	primary	$3/4$	(19)	$2^1/_4$	(57)	$36^1/_8$	(918)	
NNN	1	scroll board	primary	$3/4$	(19)	$12^1/_8$	(308)	34	(864)	$1^1/_4$" (32mm) tenon both ends
PPP	1	bottom rail	primary	$3/4$	(19)	$1^1/_4$	(32)	34	(864)	$1^1/_4$" (32mm) tenon both ends
QQQ	2	vertical dividers	pri/sec	$5/8$	(16)	$9^1/_4$	(235)	$24^1/_4$	(616)	
RRR	1	plate shelf	pri/sec	$5/8$	(16)	$8^3/_4$	(222)	$22^3/_4$	(578)	
SSS	6	side cubbyhole shelves	pri/sec	$3/8$	(10)	$8^3/_4$	(222)	6	(152)	profiled front
TTT	7	top cubbyhole dividers	pri/sec	$1/4$	(6)	$9^1/_4$	(235)	$4^1/_2$	(114)	profiled front
ARCHED TOP DOORS										
UUU	3	door stiles	primary	$3/4$	(19)	$2^1/_2$	(64)	$29^5/_8$	(753)	
VVV	1	left door, right stile	primary	$3/4$	(19)	$2^7/_8$	(73)	$29^5/_8$	(753)	
WWW	2	door bottom rails	primary	$3/4$	(19)	$2^1/_2$	(64)	$13^1/_2$	(343)	$1^1/_4$" (32mm) tenon both ends
XXX	2	door top rails	primary	$3/4$	(19)	$5^1/_4$	(133)	$13^1/_2$	(343)	$1^1/_4$" (32mm) tenon both ends
YYY	2	door panels	primary	$5/8$	(16)	$11^5/_8$	(295)	$27^{15}/_{16}$	(710)	
ZZZ	2	fan blocks	primary	$1^7/_8$	(48)	$3^3/_8$	(86)	$12^1/_2$	(318)	for carving
AAAA	2	center bonnet frames	secondary	$3/4$	(19)	$11^7/_8$	(302)	$9^{13}/_{16}$	(249)	
BBBB	2	bonnet frame backs	secondary	$3/4$	(19)	$11^7/_8$	(302)	$10^1/_8$	(257)	profiled
CCCC	1	bonnet tops	Baltic birch	$1/8$	(3)	24	(610)	24	(610)	two tops from one piece
DDDD	2	scroll backers	primary	$3/4$	(19)	2	(51)	8	(203)	
EEEE	1	center backer	primary	$3/4$	(19)	3	(76)	8	(203)	
FFFF	2	gooseneck and bonnet mouldings	primary	$2^3/_4$	(70)	7	(178)	28	(711)	
DESK INTERIOR DRAWERS										
GGGG	2	lower drawer fronts	primary	$1^1/_4$	(32)	2	(51)	16	(406)	cut to fit
HHHH	2	lower drawer short sides	secondary	$3/8$	(10)	2	(51)	$8^1/_4$	(210)	
JJJJ	2	lower drawer long sides	secondary	$3/8$	(10)	2	(51)	$12^5/_8$	(321)	
KKKK	2	lower drawer backs	secondary	$3/8$	(10)	$1^1/_2$	(38)	$13^1/_8$	(333)	
LLLL	2	upper drawer fronts	primary	$1^1/_4$	(32)	$1^{13}/_{16}$	(46)	16	(406)	cut to fit
MMMM	2	inner drawer short side	secondary	$3/8$	(10)	$1^{13}/_{16}$	(46)	$7^1/_2$	(191)	
NNNN	2	inner drawer long side	secondary	$3/8$	(10)	$1^{13}/_{16}$	(46)	$9^3/_8$	(238)	

inches (millimeters)

REFERENCE	QUANTITY	PART	STOCK	THICKNESS	(mm)	WIDTH	(mm)	LENGTH	(mm)	COMMENTS
PPPP	2	inner drawer back	secondary	$3/8$	(10)	$1^5/_{16}$	(33)	$6^3/_8$	(162)	
QQQQ	2	outer drawer short sides	secondary	$3/8$	(10)	$1^{13}/_{16}$	(46)	$9^1/_2$	(241)	
RRRR	2	outer drawer long sides	secondary	$3/8$	(10)	$1^{13}/_{16}$	(46)	$11^7/_8$	(302)	
SSSS	2	outer drawer backs	secondary	$3/8$	(10)	$1^5/_{16}$	(33)	$6^5/_{16}$	(160)	
TTTT	2	interior drawer bottoms	secondary	$1/4$	(6)	$12^1/_2$	(318)	28	(711)	cut to fit
UUUU	1	top section back	secondary	$5/8$	(16)	30	(762)	$35^1/_4$	(895)	many pieces
VVVV	1	lower section back	secondary	$5/8$	(16)	$35^1/_8$	(892)	$36^7/_8$	(937)	
FINIAL PIECES										
WWWW	2	blocks	primary	$1^3/_8$	(35)	$1^3/_8$	(35)	$1^1/_4$	(32)	cut to fit
XXXX	3	caps	primary	$1/4$	(6)	$2^1/_8$	(54)	$2^1/_8$	(54)	
YYYY	3	urns	primary	3	(76)	3	(76)	3	(76)	
ZZZZ	3	flame finials	primary	$1^1/_4$	(32)	$1^1/_4$	(32)	$5^3/_4$	(146)	

HARDWARE & SUPPLIES

6 semi-bright large drawer pulls, Horton Brass C602L

2 semi-bright small drawer pulls, Horton Brass C602S

4 semi-bright drawer escutcheons, Horton Brass C602SE

2 $3/4$" (19mm) semi-bright lid support knobs, Horton Brass H-42

1 semi-bright desk hinge, Horton Brass H-68

1 semi-bright desk lid escutcheon, Horton Brass C602LE

1 plain brass desk lid lock, Horton Brass LK-20

1 semi-bright lock strike, Horton Brass SP-2

3 semi-bright drawer escutcheons, Horton Brass H-67

1 plain brass door lock, Horton Brass LK-9

1 semi-bright lock strike, Horton Brass SP-3

8 $1/2$" (13mm) semi-bright interior drawer knobs, Horton Brass H-42

2 polished door "H" hinges, Ball and Ball H19-076

1 polished brass prospect door hinge, Rockler #32949

1 prospect door lock, Rockler #15190

1 solid brass elbow door catch, Rockler #10893

Begin this piece by milling the desk section case bottom, case sides and case top to size according to the cutting list. The joinery work begins with the case bottom; lay out and create the pins for the dovetail joints. For this operation, I like to use a jigsaw and chisels. In this photo the face, or exterior, of the case bottom is down toward the bench, and the left edge is the front of the case bottom.

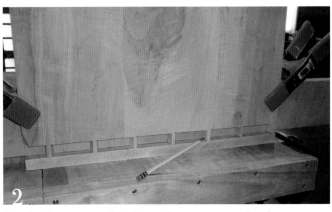

Use the pins you created in the case bottom as a template for one case side's matching tails. Position the pieces with the case side face against the bench and the case bottom's face side toward you. If you clamp a straightedge to the case bottom you can slide the case bottom into position more easily. Align the edges and the fronts of the pieces, then transfer the layout onto the case sides. A sharp pencil or marking knife will insure an accurate layout mark.

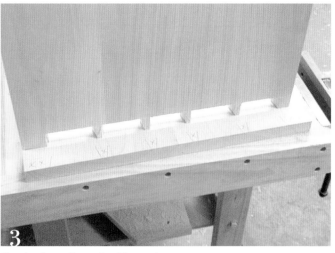

Cut the dovetails on the side panel.

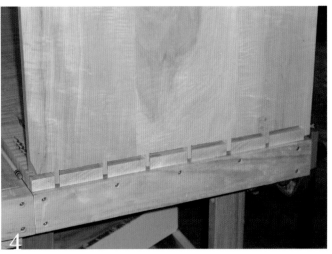

Complete the fit of the joint. Repeat steps 2 and 3 for the other case side, then complete the fit of that joint.

Lay out the pins in the case top.

Make the cuts that define the sides of the joint with a dovetail saw. Because these are half-blind dovetails, you need to overcut the lines. I extend these cuts to about the 2" (51mm) line as shown. Overcutting helps in the removal of the waste material and is present in most antique furniture pieces.

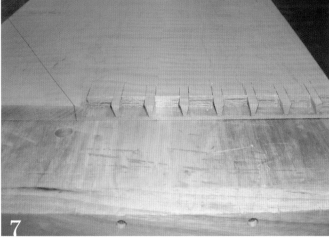

Finish the dovetail sockets, making sure to pare the bottoms level and to slightly undercut the backs (end grain).

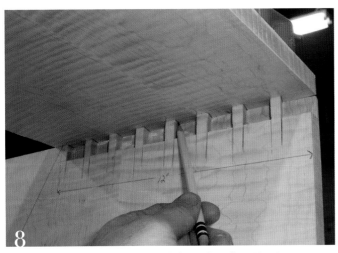

8 Scribe the case top for the half-blind dovetails and position it onto the case sides. Carefully reach into the sockets and transfer the layout onto the case top. A sharp pencil will do the job. Try to mark each line in a single pass.

9 Remove the waste material, the pin area, to create the dovetails. Test-fit the joint and make any necessary adjustments.

10

Lay out the locations for the drawer dividers in both case sides. It is important to have mirror images on the two case sides.

11 With the case top dovetails complete, cut the slope of the case sides; this is the angle of the closed desk lid. Use a jigsaw to rough the cut, and finish it with a straightedge and a pattern bit for a smooth cut.

12 Fit the case top onto one of the case sides and transfer the angle of the cut made on the case sides in step 11.

Set the table saw blade to the angle that is perpendicular to the line you transferred onto the case top in step 12. This is the first cut to make on the case top. Notice that to make this cut, you need to stand the case top vertically on the table.

Reposition the fence and blade, and make the second cut on the case top. The front edge of the case top should now have the necessary angle to match the case side cuts and have the corresponding perpendicular cut that will allow for installation of the desk lid lock's strike plate.

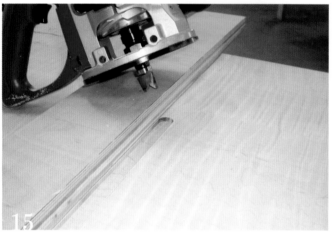

Disassemble the case, and begin making the joinery cuts in one case side. Use a straightedge that is clamped in place along with a ¾" (19mm) pattern bit to make the groove for the writing surface.

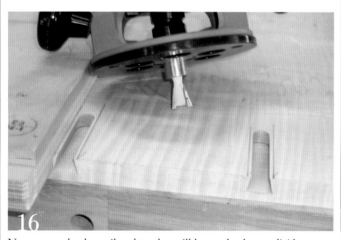

Next up are the dovetail sockets that will house the drawer dividers and the rear divider. The setup here uses a ¾" (19mm) outside diameter bushing in conjunction with a ¾"-diameter (19mm) dovetail bit. The bushing rides along the straight-edged jig and positions the socket in the middle of your layout. Set the cut depth at ½" (13mm) and cut for each drawer divider and rear divider. The bottom divider is fit between the sides.

Shown is one case side with all the joinery operations complete. Repeat steps 15 and 16 to complete the joinery in the second case side. Remember that you need to have mirror images!

With the joinery complete, make a rabbet at the back edge of each case side for the backboards. This is a two-step operation. First, set the fence for a ¾"-wide (19mm) cut, raise the blade to ⁷⁄₁₆" (11mm), and make a cut with the case sides riding flat on the table saw top.

Next readjust the blade height to match that of the first cut; the top of the blade should just kiss the upper edge of the first cut. Then set the fence to ⁵⁄₁₆" (8mm) and make the second cut as shown, forming the rabbet.

Mill the writing surface then lay out the sliding dovetails that will accept the vertical dividers that separate the lid supports from the top drawer. Make this slot just as you did in step 16 for the slots for the drawer dividers and the rear dividers. The area to the left of the layout is the section that slides into the groove in the case sides. Complete this work on the underside of the writing surface!

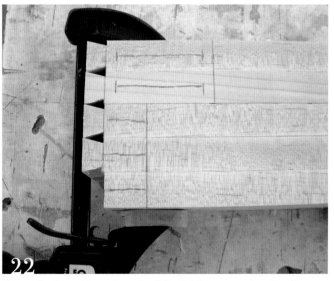

Begin the work on the front and rear dividers. Mill the pieces — along with an additional piece to be used to set up the cut — to size, then set up the router table with the same dovetail bit that you used to cut the slots. Set the bit for height first, and then position the fence for the cut width. (I ran the cut with the stock between the fence and bit for clarity in this photo. You should bury the bit in an auxiliary fence to make the cut.)

Create the dovetails on the ends of the dividers; remember that the bottom divider does not get dovetailed ends. Lay out and cut the mortises for the drawer runners. The top, front and rear dividers are laid out wider to allow the lid supports to operate on the same drawer runners the top drawer uses.

23

Cut the mortises ¼" (6mm) wide × ½" (13mm) deep.

24

Once the top divider is complete, slip it into position, use a square to locate the bottom edge of the dovetail slot for the vertical dividers and make the slot as you did in step 16. Measure, cut and create the dovetail ends on the vertical dividers as shown in step 21.

Begin to assemble the desk section case. Apply glue to the pins of the case bottom, and slide the parts together.

25

26

Position the writing surface, and apply a small amount of glue at the front edge only. This will hold the front in place and push any seasonal movement to the back of the case.

27

Install the dividers into the desk section case. Add glue to the dovetails and the slots. Do not glue the rear divider; that will need to be pulled out to install the drawer runners. Cut the bottom dividers to fit snugly in the case, and attach it with a thin bead of glue and screws from the underside of the case. (I use No.8 × 1¼" [32mm] flat-head wood screws.) Do not glue the case top into the case at this time!

28

The desk section case is assembled!

30

31

Glue the drawer runners in the front mortise, then slide the rear divider into position with glue in the dovetail socket. Next you need to space the drawer guide for the lid support's width. Add glue to the drawer guide, and hold it in place with spring clamps until dry. The rest of the drawer runners can now be installed. Glue the front mortise and tenon, and attach the drawer runner to the case side with nails (Clout, N-7) through the holes, making sure to align the drawer runners with the drawer dividers for a level drawer area.

29

Get ready to make the drawer runners by setting the blade height to ¼" (6mm) with the fence set to cut a ½" (13mm) tenon. Run the pieces, making the cuts on each face surface. Cut the runners for the lower drawers on these two faces only; the upper drawer runners need a cut on all four faces of the piece. Refer to the layout of the mortises in step 23.

The runners for the top drawer also need a 1"-long (25mm) tenon at the other end that will slide into the rear drawer runners. With the tenon shoulders defined, make the cheek cuts on each tenon. (I use a shop-made tenoning fixture at the table saw as shown.) Make a 45° cut at the rear end of the 1" (25mm) drawer runners, then predrill a ³⁄₁₆" (5mm) hole.

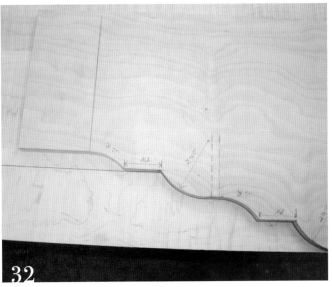

32

Make the plywood pattern shown here. You will use it a number of times throughout the project. (See the plans on the accompanying DVD.)

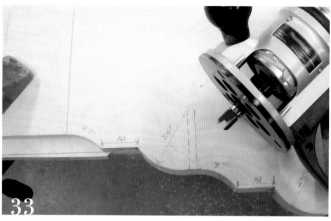

Cut the interior base to size and fit it into the desk opening. Layout the design from the pattern, then cut the design with a pattern bit against the pattern. You will notice that the pattern has one additional curve that the interior base does not have, the curve back to the horizontal dividers. Extend that line across the base to connect with the other end of the base. Repeat the cut on the other end, then run the edge with a classical ogee bit.

Temporarily attach the interior base in the desk section case, then use a ½" (13mm) pattern bit to cut the dado for the vertical dividers. Using a piece of plywood as a template cut to the correct size (13¼" [337mm]) will insure that the location of the dado is the same with each cut. Leave the dado cut ¼" (6mm) short of the width of the vertical divider.

Flip the desk onto its top and repeat the cuts for the vertical dividers. Use the same plywood template from step 34 to insure accuracy.

Notch the front edges of the vertical dividers to fit into the opening. Note: Anywhere that I needed to glue panels for this interior, I attached a primary wood to a secondary wood to be at the rear of the panel. This is denoted in the cutting list as primary/secondary.

Begin to cut the dadoes for the horizontal dividers with the case on its side. To achieve the spacing that is needed for the lower divider, install a ⅜" (10mm) straight bit into a trim router and space the cut with a piece of ¼" (6mm) plywood. Running against the plywood puts the cut in the correct position. You may need a different setup to locate the dado. Once the first cut is made, fit a scrap piece into the cut and allow the router to run against that scrap to locate the second dado.

Make the cuts on the drawer side of the vertical dividers in the same manner. Remember to stay ¼" (6mm) less than the width of the piece that is to be installed in that dado. Repeat steps 37 and 38 for the other side of the case.

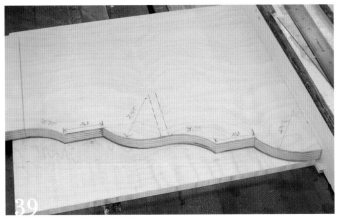

39

Because you will step back with each level to make a cathedral interior, it is necessary to push the pattern of the vertical dividers sideways, or to the outside of the desk, by ¼" (6mm) with each level. Using your pattern, slide a ¼" (6mm) spacer in, as shown, then mark the pattern on the two level 1 horizontal dividers. Make these two dividers.

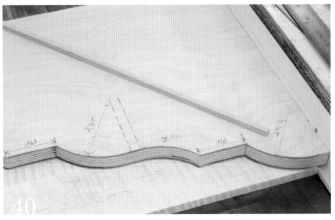

40

Remove the ¼" (6mm) spacer and use a ½" (13mm) spacer for the level 2 horizontal dividers. Make these two pieces.

41

Cut close to the layout lines on one horizontal divider, then use the plywood pattern and a pattern bit to trim the horizontal dividers to the design. Then run the classical ogee bit. The bearing will need to run against the pattern to make this profile. Repeat this process on the other three horizontal dividers.

42

Notch the ends, and slide the horizontal dividers into the case to test the fit. Remove the horizontal dividers for further processing.

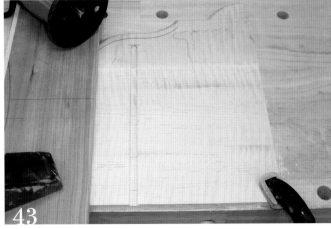

43

On the top side of the level 1 horizontal dividers make a dado for the level 2 vertical dividers, which split the level into two drawers. That dado is exactly in the middle, it is ⅜" (10mm) wide, and it is ⅛" (3mm) deep.

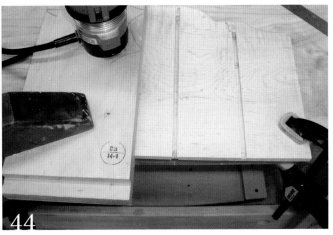

44

The work on the level 2 horizontal dividers is more involved. You can see the corresponding ⅜" (10mm) cut in the bottom of this piece for the level 2 vertical divider, and the dadoes must be laid out and cut for the cubbyhole dividers as well. Those dadoes are ¼" (6mm) wide × ⅛" (3mm) deep and equally spaced in the openings. Stay back ¾" (19mm) from the front edge of the level 2 horizontal dividers.

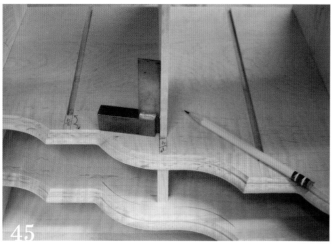

Slide the horizontal dividers back into the case. Cut a scrap piece of material that is ¼" (6mm) thick and just tall enough to slide into the cubbyhole dadoes and fit snugly against the underside of the case top. To insure a 90° angle to the cubbyhole dividers, slide the scrap into each dado and transfer the layout lines to the underside of the case top. Remove the case top and cut the dadoes for the cubbyhole dividers. Glue the case top into the case.

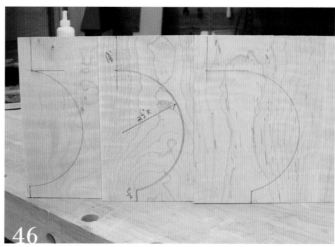

The top edges of the cubbyhole dividers all come to the same location in the underside of the case top for an even valance. Conversely, the bottom edge of each set of cubbyhole dividers is different based on the depth of the horizontal dividers at the dado. Measure the length of the dado at the top, add ¼" (6mm), then draw a line down 1⅜" (35mm). Do this for the bottom edge and make the line up ½" (13mm). Make a half circle (2½" [64mm] radius) in the two center cubbyhole dividers, one for each side of the interior. Cut those cubbyhole dividers, sand the front edges and use them as patterns for the other two cubbyhole dividers.

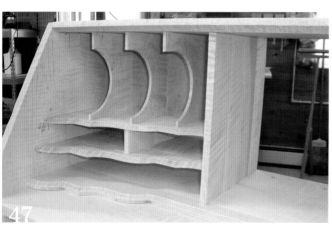

This is how the cubbyhole dividers look. Now remove the vertical dividers and lay out three equal sections for the secret compartments; each compartment is divided by a ¼" (6mm) shelf. Reinstall the vertical dividers and add the vertical divider front to each edge as shown in step 48.

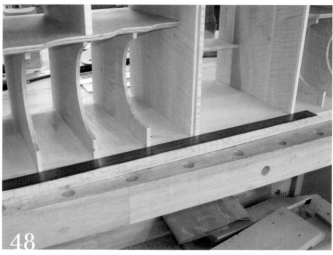

Use a straightedge to make sure that all the pieces line up at the valance area.

Cut and fit each valance between the cubbyhole dividers, trace the profile onto the pieces, then cut and sand the profile. Glue each valance in place so that it is even with the front edge of each cubbyhole divider. Once the valances are in position, add a valance block behind each valance.

tip

Set up a straightedge at the band saw and make a small slot at the front edge of each valance. This slot acts as a glue reservoir, which keeps any squeeze-out off the face of the piece.

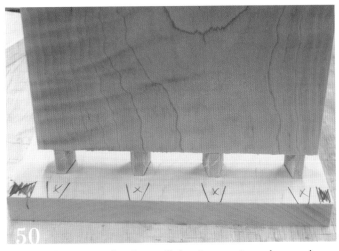

50
To begin the prospect door box, mill the pieces to size and create the pins in the top and bottom. The shaded areas are ¾" (19mm) (shown on the left) for the door to close against and ¼" (6mm) (shown on the right) for the backboard of the prospect door box.

51
Complete the dovetails for the prospect door box. Glue the prospect door box together, making sure it is square.

52
Add the front face pieces to the prospect door box next. Use duct tape as a clamp. Also, cut and fit the back for the prospect door box.

53
Shown here are the pieces that make up the hidden drawer boxes. Create the pins in the fronts and backs of the drawer boxes, and attach the drawer bottoms with brads. Check how each drawer box fits into the area that is behind the prospect door box.

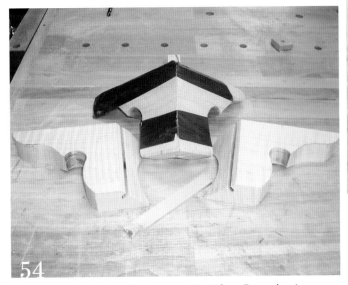

54
It's time to make the feet. Follow steps 28-33 from Pennsylvania Chest on Chest.

55

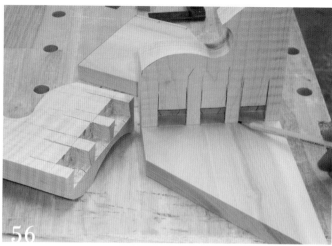

56

Dovetail the side feet to the rear feet. Speed up the cutting of the dovetail sockets by hogging out waste material at the drill press. Cut to the scribe line — the thickness of the rear foot — then complete the socket with chisels.

Set the completed side foot onto the rear foot and transfer the layout. The pins are in the side feet, so create the tails in the rear feet. Cut to the lines at the band saw, and use chisels to remove the waste material. Test the fit, make any necessary adjustments, then glue the assembly.

57

Finish shaping the paired feet with hand tools, and sand them up to 180-grit sandpaper.

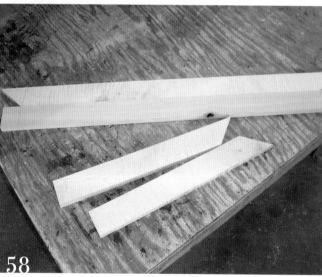

58

59

Mill the parts for the base frame according to the cutting list. To ensure that you have the correct length for the base frame back, mark the two tenons on one end of the piece and position that mark at the inner angle cut of the base frame front. Then, mark the point where the opposite inner angle meets the base frame back. This will ensure a square base frame.

Cut both ends of the base frame front and one end of each base frame side for No.20 biscuits. The remaining end of each side is to have a mortise for the tenons on the base frame back.

First glue the mortise and tenon joint together, then glue the front corners with the biscuits. Position clamps as shown so that you can regulate the clamping and pull the mitered corners together tightly. Check the frame for square. Set it aside to dry.

With the base frame dry, sand both sides and attach the foot assemblies. Make sure to have the feet positioned correctly so that the edge of each foot rolls into the base frame. Pay attention to the positions. The foot assemblies may slide while being clamped.

Add blocking to both the corner of the foot as well as the intersection of the foot and the frame. The best method to avoid cross-grain blocking is to use a series of blocks that have the grain staggered. A hot glue pot and glue is advantageous in this process. Glue the blocks together, changing the grain direction with each block. Once the glue is set, straighten the blocking and glue it into position. The other blocks, between the foot and the base frame, do not require the staggered grain treatment. Attach them with glue and brads, if necessary.

With the foot assemblies attached to the base frame, create the profile on the base frame edges. Pay close attention to the ends of the base frame sides as you use your router. It is easy to roll around onto the back corner of the base frame; this unsightly error cannot be remedied.

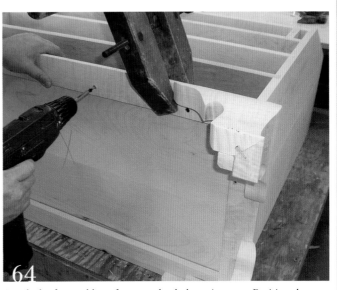

Attach the feet and base frame to the desk section case. Position the base frame to the desk section case, add glue along the front edge, and make the attachment by using screws at the front. Use nails along the sides and back. The nails will allow seasonal movement of the bottom panel.

65 Cut and fit the transition mouldings.

66 Time to build the drawers! Build these drawers exactly like those in the bonnet top high chest. (See Massachusetts High Chest, steps 67-76, then steps 83-84.)

67 To create the support face, begin by profiling the edges. Then, set the table saw to create a ½" (13mm) tenon in the center of each support face.

68 Next, trim the waste, leaving a ⁵⁄₁₆" (8mm) lip on the support face. I have installed a scrap of ¼" (6mm) plywood on the saw's table top to provide a zero-clearance throat.

69 Mill the lid supports to size based on the opening in your desk. It is important to have a good fit; otherwise the support will sag when extended completely. Cut a corresponding groove into one end of each lid support. Because the support face is slightly taller than the lid support, you will need to trim the top edge of the support face tenon.

tip

The lid support faces need to be edged with the same ³⁄₁₆" (5mm) beading bit so that the profiles match. With such a small piece, use double-stick tape to hold the stock while the edges are moulded.

When you have completed the finish on the unit you will need to attach the support stops to the lid supports. The placement of these support stops should allow the lid supports to be pulled out past the lip of the desk lid as the support stops make contact with the inside of the desk section vertical dividers. Place one support stop on the interior side of each lid support.

Make a mock-up of the desk lid to check the fit. This insures that the rabbet on the edges is correct and that the width of the desk lid is also right. Once confirmed, mill the parts for the desk lid.

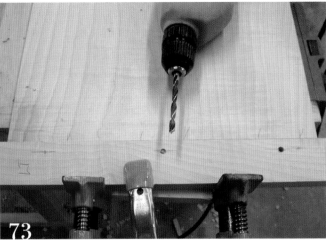

Begin by creating a 1⅛" (29mm) tenon on each end of the desk lid in the same manner as you made the tenons on the drawer runners. To strengthen the joint, cut the multiple-tenon layout, as shown. Then, create the ¼" × ⅜" (6mm x 10mm) groove in the breadboard ends at the table saw. Lay out and cut the mortise area for the tenons. The center mortise is tightly fit to the tenon, whereas the outer two mortises are cut slightly larger than the tenons to allow for expansion and contraction of the desk lid.

Fit the breadboard ends to the desk lid and clamp the unit tight. Drill a ¼" (6mm) hole within the width of each tenon. It helps to mark the tenon width near the edge of the desk lid. Add a piece of scrap to the underside of the assembly to reduce any blowout that might occur. Remove the breadboard ends. Add glue to the center mortise and tenon only, then reinstall the ends on the desk lid. Install the ¼" × ¼" (6mm x 6mm) hardwood pegs in the holes and sand flush.

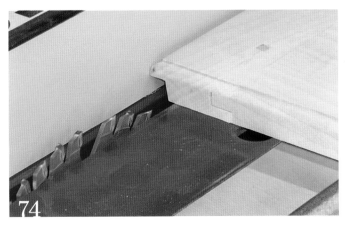

Trim the breadboard ends to fit the desk lid, and profile all four edges of the unit with the 3/16" (5mm) beading bit. Next create the rabbet on the ends and the top edge of the desk lid only. While this rabbet is made in the same two-step process, it is a bit different: Angle the blade for the second cut to 20° as shown. This has two purposes. It allows the desk lid a better fit, especially at the top edge, and it matches the angle on the desk lid lock that you will install later.

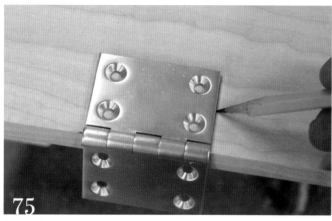

75 Set the hinges into the writing surface and space them about 6" (152mm) from the case sides. Draw an outline of the hinge, and set the depth of cut of the router to the thickness of the hinges. Before routing, set the edges of the hinge area with a chisel and make a small cut in the front edge of the writing surface to limit the chance of tear-out during routing. Clean out the outlined area and fit the hinge's leaf into the writing surface.

76 Set the desk lid into position and onto the lid supports. Place a folded business card between the desk lid and the writing surface for spacing, then mark the second leaf on the desk lid. Repeat step 75 to install the hinge. Once the hinge installation is complete, install the half-mortise lock.

77 Except for the interior drawers and backboards, the lower desk section is complete!

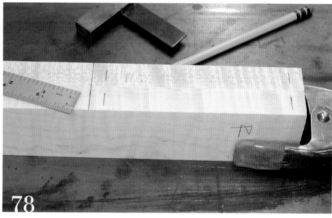

78 Begin work on the upper section, or the bookcase, of the piece. Mill the parts to size according to the cutting list, and lay out the locations and widths of the mortises in the face frame stiles. Each mortise is $\frac{1}{4}$" (6mm) wide and $1\frac{1}{4}$" (32mm) deep. The length of each mortise is $\frac{3}{4}$" (19mm) less than the width of the bottom rail and the scroll board end (after you have laid out the design from the plans), respectively.

79 Lay out the plan for the scroll board from the accompanying DVD. Create the tenons on the bottom rail and scroll board as you did on the desk lid. Remove the waste material by sawing to the shoulder and chiseling from the shoulder.

80 Use a miter saw to make the straight cuts that begin the cutting of the scroll board to pattern.

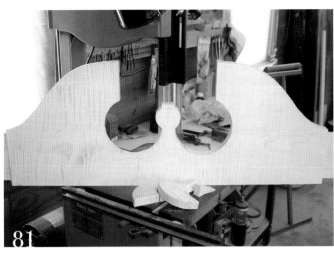

Finish the scroll board profile at the band saw, and sand the edges.

Test the fit of the joinery and remember to cut a small-radius profile at the top edge of the face frame stiles. Be sure to continue the sweep of the top edge of the scroll board. Assemble the face frame, and allow the glue to dry.

Cut the arches that will expose the fan carvings into the scroll board and provide recessed areas where the doors can fit. Begin 2¼" (57mm) from one face frame stile and cut one on a 7¼" (184mm) radius. The vertical line shown is located at the center of the door opening, or 7⅞" (200mm) from the face frame stile. Make a pattern for this arch, rough-cut the waste, then use the pattern along with a router and pattern bit to cut both openings, one over each door area.

Prepare to mill the bookcase section case sides by laying out the case shelf locations. Remember that the case middle shelf is only ⅝" (16mm) thick. Use a straightedge and a pattern bit to make the cuts, then create a two-step rabbet for the backboards at the rear edge of each piece. Make sure to have a mirrored pair.

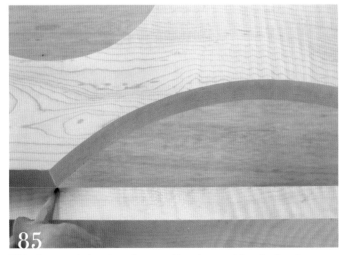

Slide the case shelves into the case sides, then position the face frame assembly against the case. Mark the endpoints of the arches on the case in the scroll board. These marks become the defining edges of the arch cuts that go into the case top shelf for the fan carvings.

86 Lay out the arch in the case top shelf. The arch should extend into the case top shelf 1¾" (45mm) and touch each mark made in step 85.

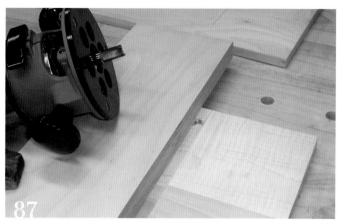

87 Before breaking down the unit, measure in 5½" (140mm) from each case side and lay out the locations for the vertical dividers. Dadoes need to be cut into the top side of the case bottom shelf and the underside of the case middle shelf to receive these vertical dividers. Make the cuts 9" (229mm) in from the back edges of the case shelves.

88 Lay out and cut the dadoes for the plate shelf, which runs between the two vertical dividers.

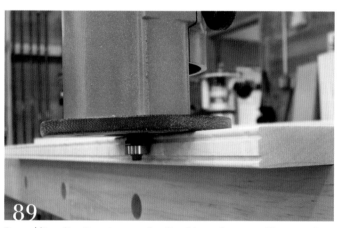

89 Run a ⅛"-radius (3mm) corner beading bit on the top and bottom of the front edges of these parts: middle shelf, the two vertical dividers and the plate shelf. Run the radius only on the bottom of the front edge of the case top shelf and on the top edge of the case bottom shelf.

90 Notch the front edges of the vertical dividers and the plate shelf to fit over the dadoes; the dadoes are run ¼" (6mm) short of the overall widths of the pieces. Slide the unit together, and begin the layout of the side cubbyhole shelves. Use a spacer to insure accurate location for the first shelf.

91 To make dadoes for the side cubbyhole shelves, make the cut for the first side cubbyhole shelf at the line from step 90, then slide a scrap piece into the dado and lay out the next location. Repeat this process for each side cubbyhole shelf location in the insides of the case sides as well as the outer faces of the vertical dividers.

92

On the top face of the case middle shelf, lay out and cut the dadoes for the top cubbyhole dividers. These should be equally spaced across the entire length of the case middle shelf.

94

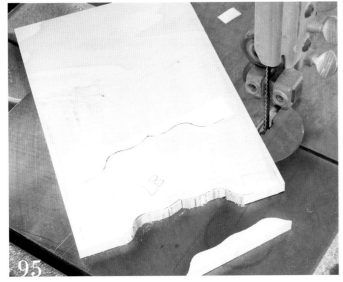

95

Mark the edge profile on the cubbyhole shelves from a pattern included in the DVD plans, making sure that the pattern is centered between the notch areas. Cut that profile at a band saw and sand up to 180-grit sandpaper. Work each shelf into the unit, and mark the position on the back edge for reference.

93

To insure correct placement into the underside of the case top shelf, slip the case shelves into the case sides again and use a a small square along with a scrap that fits into the dado to mark each dado location. Remove the case top shelf and cut these dadoes. Stay back ⅝" (16mm) from the front edge of the case top shelf.

Time for some assembly. Attach the plate shelf into the vertical dividers with screws, then attach that unit into the case bottom and middle shelves in the same manner. Install the three case shelves into the case sides by driving brads into the shelves and case sides from the underside of each shelf. Next, mill the material for the side cubbyhole shelves and slide each into place, tight against the dadoes. Mark the sides of each cubbyhole shelf to locate the notches that will allow the piece to cover the dadoes.

96

It's time for more assembly! Add a small line of glue to the case sides' front edge, and attach the face frame unit to the case. You can add glue to the case bottom shelf, but remember that the case bottom shelf is set ¼" (6mm) above the face frame bottom rail. Watch for squeeze-out!

97

On the plate shelf create a groove that is 1½" (38mm) in from the back edge. I like to do this step after the plate shelf is installed so that I can run from side to side with my router base acting as a stop. You can complete this step prior to installation, if you like.

98

Mill, fit and profile the front edges of the top cubbyhole dividers. The layout, as shown in the picture, depends on the location in the unit because of the arched area for the fan carving. However, the overall width (watch the grain direction) is consistent because each top cubbyhole divider extends to the same location on the bottom edge.

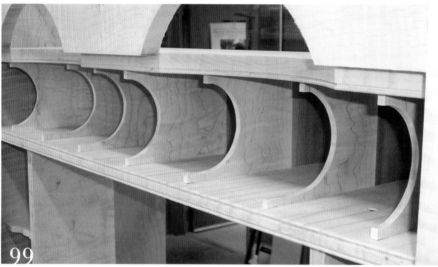

99

Here is the finished look of the top cubbyholes. Notice how the top cubbyhole dividers curve around the arched openings.

100

Turning your attention to the arched top doors, which rabbet at the middle, mill the material according to the cutting list. Note that the left door is the rabbeted door, whereas the right door is lipped. Therefore, the left door's right stile is wider than the other door stiles.

101

Run the ³⁄₁₆" (5mm) beading profile on the interior edge of all the door-frame parts.

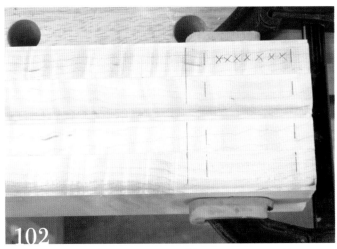

Lay out and cut the ¼"-wide (6mm) × 1¼"-deep (32mm) × 1¾"-long (45mm) mortises in the door stiles that will receive the tenons of the door rails. The full lines denote the innermost edge of the door rails.

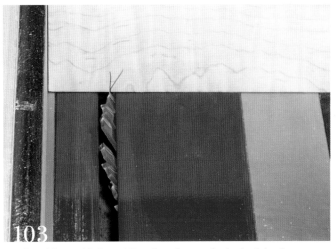

Set the table saw blade to 45° and mark onto the back of the door rails and door stiles the bottom edge or the innermost edge of the layout lines from step 102. Locate the mark to the blade tooth so that the tip of the tooth touches the line just as the blade goes below the tabletop. On this door, there is one setup for the rails and one setup for the stiles. (Shown on the accompanying DVD.)

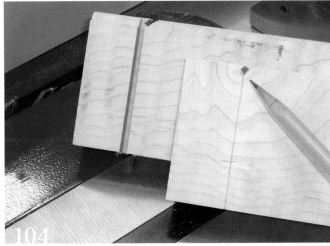

Reset the blade to 90° and raise the cut to ¼" (6mm) to make the shoulder cuts on the front and back of the door rails. Position the fence so the cut gets made just at the point of the 45° cut, as shown.

Without resetting the fence, raise the blade to ⅜" (10mm) and make a third shoulder cut. This time cut at the angled cut or on the interior edge of the door rails.

Adjust the fence toward the blade ³⁄₁₆" (5mm) and make the last shoulder cut. This cut should be on the outside edge. This will create the haunched tenon to fill in for the ¼" (6mm) groove that you will make to hold the door raised panel. The groove is to be ⅜" (10mm) deep and you will remove the ³⁄₁₆" (5mm) beading on the door stiles (see step 107), so you need to adjust only the difference, or ³⁄₁₆" (5mm).

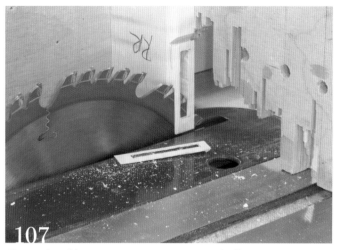

107 Change the table saw setup so you can remove the ³⁄₁₆" (5mm) bead profile on the door stiles up to the angled cut, as shown. You will need to use a tenoning jig; mine is a shop-made jig.

Remove the waste area of the tenons or make the cheek cuts using the tenon cutter. Cut one side, then reverse the piece to make the second cut. This will insure that the tenon is located in the middle of the piece.

109 Finish the edge cuts for the door bottom rails at a band saw. Notice the haunch at the bottom edge of the tenon away from the angled cut.

110 Removing the waste area on the door top rails is a bit more involved. The majority of the waste can be removed the same way you removed the waste area on the scroll board in step 79. The remaining area needs to be removed at a band saw to leave the haunch that will be seen at the top edge of the door.

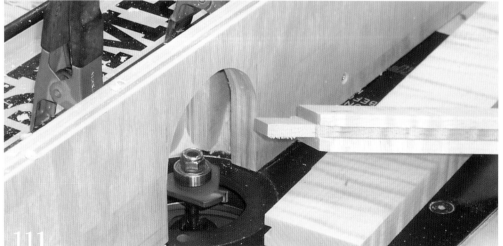

111 Set up to cut the grooves in the centers of all the door rails and door stiles. I use a three-wing cutter at a router table. You can also do this operation at a table saw.

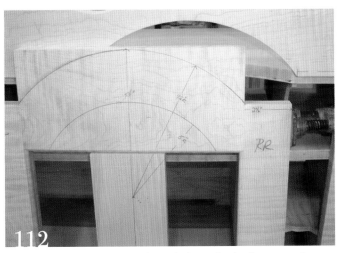

112

Assemble the doors to lay out the arched cuts for the door top rail. Draw a center line through the door top rails and into a scrap piece of wood. Use a compass to draw an arc that has a 7½" (191mm) radius and intersects the two points where the door stiles and door rails meet. Then, readjust and draw a 5"-radius (127mm) arc from the same point.

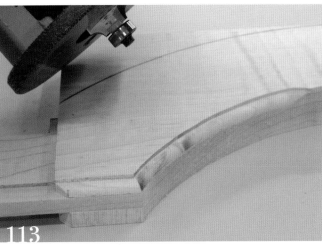

113

Cut the 5"-radius (127mm) line at a band saw and sand the cut smooth. Now create the 3/16" (5mm) bead on the edge you just cut. To do this with the same beading bit, you need to fill in the area that has already been grooved for your door panel. Fit a piece to each side and create the bead profile. Then, use the three-wing cutter to make the groove in the arched interior edge of the door top rail, and make the cut at the outside radius or top edge of the door.

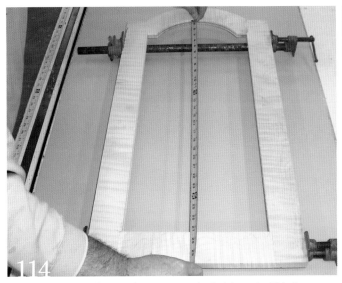

114

Assemble the door frames, then measure the height and width for the door panel. You will get a more accurate reading if you work on the back face of the door frames. Add 5/8" (16mm) to both measurements to gain the overall size of the door panel. Mill the door panels to size, then lay out the areas that will be in the grooves you made into the door rails and door stiles, especially the top shoulders.

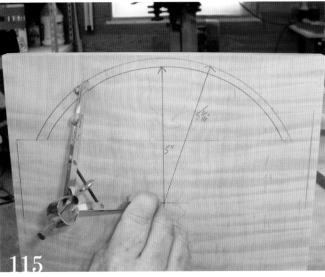

115

The outside radius of the door panel is also the inside radius of the door top rail. Lay out the arc using a 5" (127mm) radius, bringing the line to the shoulders on each side. The center point should be the center of the door. Because you are adding 5/16" (8mm) to extend into the groove — one half of the 5/8" (16mm) you added — you need to also add that 5/16" (8mm) to the top edge of the arched door panel.

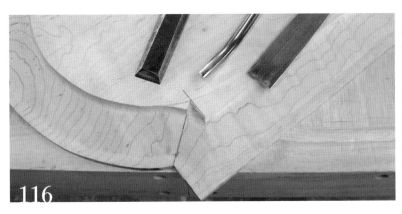

116

Cut the door panel's raised edges. This can be accomplished with a shaper, a router table or some other method that you use. To finish the door panel you need to do handwork at the intersection of the arch and the shoulders. Continue the line of the inside cut of your door panel edge so it touches the shoulder line. Work tightly into the corner while maintaining the plane of each side of the edge. Assemble the doors. Use glue in the mortise and tenon, but not on the panel.

Here is a tricky part. Remember from step 100 that the left door is to be rabbeted and that the right door is to be lipped and extended over the left door. To create the rabbeted door you will need an ovolo bit setup in the router table; the radius needs to be the same as a matching beading bit (I used one with a $\frac{1}{4}$" [6mm] radius). Bury the bit in an auxiliary fence, make the cut with the door facedown, and leave $\frac{5}{16}$" (8mm) of flat after the beaded area.

Load your matching beading bit into a router and make the edge cuts around the remaining areas of both doors. Make sure to set the height and to work carefully as you near the edges that have been routed with the ovolo bit.

The next step is to cut the rabbet that will allow the doors to overlap the bookcase section's opening. Do this only on all edges that were cut with the beading bit. Pay close attention as you near the nonrabbeted edge of the left door. It is very easy to allow the rabbeting bit to "sneak" around the corner, causing a bad cut! Test-fit the doors and the opening and make any necessary adjustments. Look at the rounded corners where the arched top meets the shoulders. Use chisels to square the radius left from the rabbeting bit. Install a half-mortise lock, and hang the doors with H-hinge hardware.

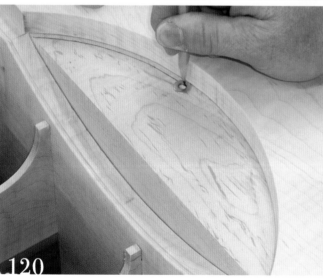

Mill the fan blocks to size. Position them in place and secure them. Mark the exact opening for reference, but when you carve the fans do not work all the way to the lines. Leave about $\frac{1}{4}$" (6mm) of space around the carved areas. I have found that a small washer works wonders: You can mark with a pencil on the inner edge of the washer, and as the washer rolls along the edge you get a perfect border.

Use carving chisels to rough out the fan area. I use a #2/20mm and #3/20mm sweep gouge for this step. The surface should be rounded from the lower edge to the top border.

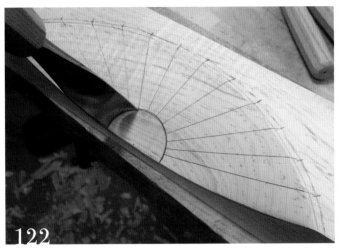

122

Level the carved area with a scraper or sander and layout the fan design onto the block. The fan has 13 rays that are equally spaced along the outer arc of the fan. The inner circle has a radius of $1\frac{3}{4}$" (45mm). Use a #7/20mm sweep gouge to set the edge around the inner circle, as shown, and then carve the lines that divide the rays by using a #15/3mm and #16/6mm V-parting tool.

123

Work the V-parting tools to about $\frac{3}{16}$" (5mm) depth, then round over each edge of the rays. (I like to use a #25/3mm sweep back bent gouge for this step.) Remember to turn your workpiece as you carve so that you carve with the grain. Going against the grain can present problems such as tear-out. You will be able to feel the grain direction as you carve. It will be harder to cut! Another helpful tip is to wet the surface to be carved for the fan. The water allows you to carve the wood more easily.

124

Do not be intimidated by these fans. They are a simple introduction to carving. Once they are complete, sand the carving smooth, and install the fans into their openings. Glue is all that is required for installation at this time.

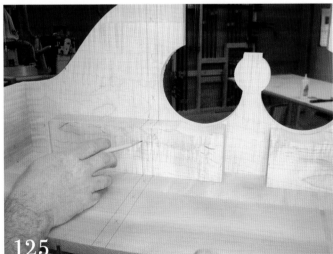

125

Shown here is the back of the fan blocks after they are installed. Notice that you need to work the area that extends into the arch of the scroll board. Also, the layout lines for the center bonnet frame are shown. This piece will notch over the fan blocks and help to secure them in the piece.

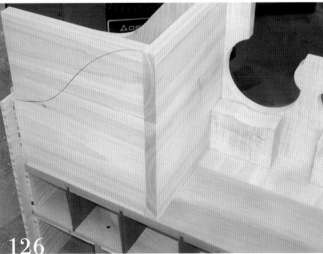

126

Cut and fit the bonnet frame back as well. This piece will have the same profile as the scroll board. Cut the piece to fit, slide it to the front or tightly against the back of the scroll board, and transfer the profile to the bonnet frame back.

127 Attach the bonnet frame pieces to the case. Attach the center bonnet frame to the scroll board with a single screw that will be behind the bonnet moulding, a screw in from the underside of the bookcase section case top shelf, and install a glue block as shown. Install the bonnet frame back with the screws from the underside and glue blocks as well, but do not use a screw through the center bonnet frame because that would be visible. Just rely on the glue blocks.

128 Cut the stock for the scroll and the center backers. Trace the profiles needed, cut to those profiles, and install the scroll backers and the center backer to the scroll board with glue and brads.

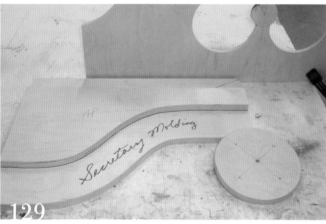

Make the bonnet mouldings. To make the necessary patterns, see Massachusetts High Chest, step 50.

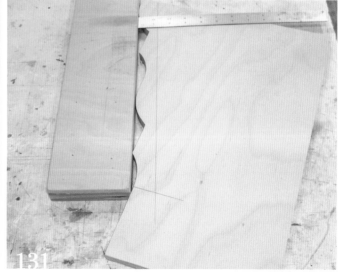

130 Make the gooseneck and straight mouldings for the bonnet top. For instructions, see Massachusetts High Chest, steps 51-63.

131 To begin the desk interior drawers, lay out the pattern from the plans on the accompanying DVD and check the thickness needed per the cutting list by laying a straightedge along the front, then measure back 1¼" (32mm). This will give you both the angle needed to cut the drawer fronts and the overall length of the drawer front material.

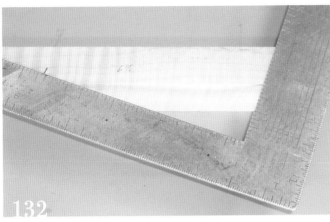

Mill the drawer front stock to size, set a miter saw to the correct angle, and make a cut at one end. Use a square to locate the cut for the other end and return to the miter saw to cut to length.

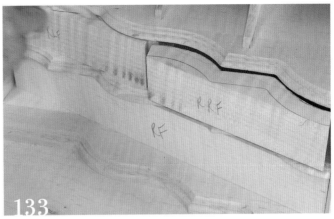

Position the drawer-front block into the opening and transfer the profile of the horizontal dividers onto the back edge of each drawer front. Cut that profile at a band saw. Reposition the piece, slide it farther into the opening, and transfer another line for the profiled drawer front. Repeat this process on each of the remaining drawer fronts.

One end of each drawer front will have a drawer side against it at 90°. The opposite end will need to be adjusted as shown. The depth of cut in from the edge is ⅜" (10mm), the thickness of the drawer sides. Make these adjustments with chisels, then lay out the dovetail sockets. On a drill press, set the angle of the bit so it corresponds to the angle cut on the drawer fronts, then cut out as much as possible with a Forstner bit. Clean up the rest of the socket using chisels.

Set the drawer front onto the drawer side after it has been scribed, and transfer the layout to create the tails. Repeat steps 134 and 135 for each desk interior drawer.

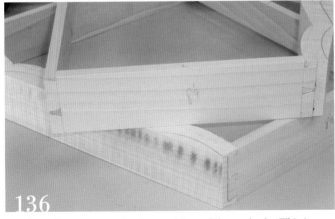

Use dovetails to connect the drawer sides and drawer backs. This is a drawer with the dovetails complete.

Disassemble the desk interior drawers and set up to cut the grooves that will hold the drawer bottoms. Use a three-wing cutter set for a ¼"-deep (6mm) cut. This can be used on the curved drawer fronts, but because of the thickness of the drawer sides, you will need to either use an auxiliary fence to reduce the depth of the cut or else make the grooves in the drawer sides at a table saw with the blade height set at ³⁄₁₆" (5mm) or half the thickness of the drawer sides. Cut, shape and sand the drawer fronts to the lines, then assemble the drawers.

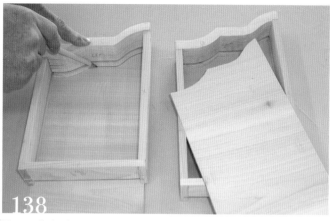

138

To install the drawer bottoms, cut the pieces to the correct width, which you measure between the grooves of the drawer sides at the drawer back. Position the assembled drawer onto the drawer bottom, trace and cut the profile of the back edge of the drawer fronts, then slip the drawer bottom into the drawer box and mark about ¼" (6mm) beyond the rear edge of the drawer back. Make the cutoff there, and install the drawer bottom with brads.

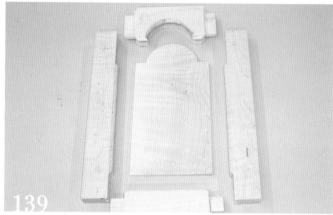

139

Make the prospect door. It is made in the same manner as the bookcase section doors with three exceptions. First, the overall size is much smaller. Second, the top rail is arched only on the lower edge, so the entire top rail is housed in the stiles. Third, the panel is flat rather than raised. All the joinery is identical. Hang the prospect door with butt hinges, and install a half-mortise lock.

140

Cut and install the finial blocks per the instructions in Massachusetts High Chest, steps 92-95. (The only lathe work in this piece is the finials.) Turn the urns according to the plans on the DVD.

141

Mill the backboards and fit them to the cases. Finish-sand the piece completely to prepare for staining.

"ROUTER BIT SPECIFIC" FENCE

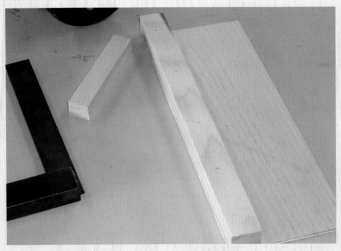

(STEP ONE) Only three pieces are needed to build a "router bit specific" straight-edged fence. You will need a piece of ¼" (6mm) plywood that is about 4" × 10" (102mm × 254mm), one piece of hardwood that is ¾" × 1" × 11" (19mm x 25mm × 279mm) for the fence, and one piece that is ¾" × ¾" × 3" (19mm × 19mm × 76mm) for the square catch. Attach the fence piece with glue and brads to the edge of the plywood that has been cut square.

(STEP TWO) Use a square to set the catch piece. It is important that the piece be exactly 90° to the fence. Attach the piece to the plywood and the fence with glue and brads.

(STEP THREE) Load the router bit into the router and, holding the base of the trim router against the fence, make a cut the entire length of the jig.

(STEP FOUR) Now, whenever you use this jig with this specific router bit, all you need to do is align the edge of the plywood with the layout line of your cut. The cut will be precisely where you planned it to be! Remember to label the appropriate router and bit on each jig you make.

BENDHEIM EAST, ARCHITECTURAL DIVISION
61 Willett Street
Passaic, NJ 07055
800-835-5304
www.bendheim.com
Restoration glass

DAVID LINDOW
527 Gravity Road
Lake Ariel, PA 18436
570-937-3301
Clockmaker

DONALD DURHAM COMPANY
Box 804-E
Des Moines, IA 50304
515-243-0491
www.waterputty.com
Durham's Rock Hard Water Putty

HORTON BRASSES INC.
49 Nooks Hill Road
Cromwell, CT 06416
800-754-9127
www.horton-brasses.com
Brass hardware

IRION LUMBER COMPANY
P.O. Box 954
Wellsboro, PA 16901-0954
570-724-1895
www.irionlumber.com
Hardwood lumber

KATHI EDWARDS
1555 McGarity Road
Temple, GA 30179
770-505-4417
Dial painter

LEE VALLEY
U.S.:
P.O. Box 1780
Ogdensburg, NY 13669-6780
800-267-8735
Canada:
P.O. Box 6295, Station J
Ottawa, ON K2A 1T4
800-267-8761
www.leevalley.com
Woodworking tool manufacturer (Veritas) and supercatalog retailer of tools, accessories, supplies and hardware.

ROCKLER WOODWORKING AND HARDWARE
4365 Willow Drive
Medina, MN 55340
800-279-4441
www.rockler.com
Hardware and router bits

WOODCRAFT SUPPLY CORP.
1177 Rosemar Road
P.O. Box 1686
Parkersburg, WV 26102
800-535-4482
www.woodcraft.com
Hardware and router bits

WOODWORKER'S EDGE
6895 Dutchland Boulevard
Middletown, OH 45044
www.woodworkersedge.com
Specialty moulding

B

Block-front chest
  background, 9
  case, 16, 20
  drawer dividers, 12-15, 19
  drawer runners, 17
  drawers, 20-23
  feet, 17-18, 19
  finishing, 23
  hardware and supplies, 11, 23
  mouldings, 16-17, 18, 19
  parts list, 11
  plan drawing, 10

C

Chest on chest
  background, 49
  case, 53-54, 60-61
  drawer dividers, 55-56, 61-62
  drawer runners, 56-57, 62
  drawers, 63-64
  feet, 58-60
  finishing, 64
  hardware and supplies, 52
  mouldings, 62-63
  parts list, 51-52
  plan drawing, 50
  quartered columns, 57-58
  wooden clips, 65
Chippendale period block-front
    chest. *See* Block-front chest
Clock. *See* Tall case clock

D

Desk and bookcase
  background, 93
  base, 104, 108-109
  bonnet, 121-122
  bookcase construction, 112-115
  bookcase doors, 116-120

  case, 97-101, 102-103
  cubby holes, 115-116
  desk lid, 110-112
  dividers, 104-106
  drawer dividers, 99-102
  drawer runners, 103
  drawers, 107, 110, 122-124
  fans, 120-121
  feet, 108, 109
  finishing, 124
  hardware and supplies, 97
  parts list, 95-97
  plan drawing, 94
  prospect door, 107, 124
  sidebar head, 125

G

Glass shelving safety tips, 3

H

High chest (highboy)
  background, 25
  base frame, 34-35
  bonnet, 38-41
  drawer dividers, 30-32, 36, 37-38
  drawer runners, 32-33, 36, 37
  drawers, 41-45
  finishing, 47
  hardware and supplies, 28
  kickers, 33
  knee blocks, 34, 45
  legs and feet, 29-30, 45
  parts list, 27-28
  plan drawing, 26
  trim, 46-47
  upper case, 35-36

M

Massachusetts block-front chest.
    See Block-front chest
Massachusetts high chest (highboy).
    See High chest (highboy)
Metric conversion chart, 2

N

New England desk and bookcase.
    See Desk and bookcase

P

Parts lists
  block-front chest, 11
  chest on chest, 51-52
  desk and bookcase, 95-97
  high chest (highboy), 27-28
  tall case clock, 69-70
Pennsylvania chest on chest. *See*
    Chest on chest
Pennsylvania tall case clock. *See*
    Tall case clock
Plan drawings
  block-front chest, 10
  chest on chest, 50
  desk and bookcase, 94
  high chest (highboy), 26
  tall case clock, 68
Power equipment safety tips, 3

R

Router bit specific fence, 125

S

Safety tips
  glass shelving, 3
  power equipment, 3
Secretary. *See* Desk and bookcase
Suppliers, 126

T

Tall case clock
  background, 67
  base, 71, 73-74
  carvings, 87-89, 90
  dial frame, 84
  face frame, 71-72, 74
  feet, 72-73
  finishing, 90
  fretwork, 81-82
  gooseneck, 78-79, 82-83, 91
  hardware and supplies, 70, 89, 90
  hood, 74-77, 81, 84-86, 89, 90
  mouldings, 79-81
  parts list, 69-70
  pediment, 77-79
  plan drawing, 68
  waist section, 73-74, 80
Tiger maple, 93
Tips
  glue reservoir, 106
  moulding edges, 110
  turnings, 91
  waste removal, 43

W

Wooden clips, 65

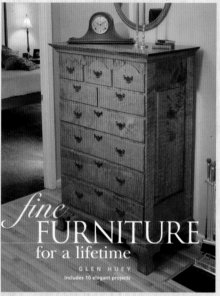
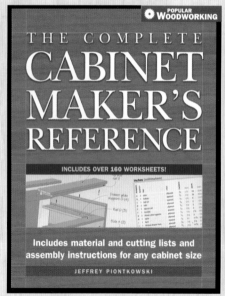
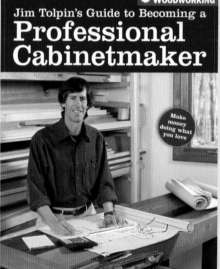